SEX, DRUGS, & SOUL

Sex, Drugs, & Soul

FINDING GRACE
IN THE SHADOW

A MEMOIR

KRISTIN
BIRDWELL

HOUNDSTOOTH
PRESS

SEX, DRUGS, & SOUL
Finding Grace in the Shadow

ISBN 978-1-5445-3077-2 *Hardcover*
      978-1-5445-3078-9 *Paperback*
      978-1-5445-3079-6 *Ebook*

To Mama, for always inspiring me to dream big.
To Daddy, for all the scenic routes.
...and for Little Tommy.

"Buy the ticket, take the ride...and if it occasionally gets a little heavier than what you had in mind, well...maybe chalk it up to forced consciousness expansion."

—Hunter S. Thompson

1

When I dreamed of seeing the world outside of the rural East Texas towns I grew up in, I never envisioned abandoning myself to do so. At twenty-one, I started dating Bradley, a handsome and charismatic, yet turbulent, man from a sugar daddy dating website who was decades my senior. And although I didn't know it at the time, our relationship was my means of seeking salvation, to dress the shame-filled spaces of my inner life as a pretty little depiction for others, to fill the void formed by my biological dad's absent affection, and mostly, to hide my true self.

I wanted everyone to only know the good parts of me. The good parts were the only parts of myself I loved, the only spaces I deemed worthy of love. I hid the doubt, the shame, the sadness, the fear, the desperation, and the destructive behaviors because somewhere along the way, I'd been conditioned to believe it wasn't safe to be vulnerable or unapologetically me. Those parts of me wouldn't be loved or appreciated; those parts of me had to be hidden.

Shortly after my birthday, I showed up on the doorstep of Bradley's Dallas mansion wearing brown, rubber flip flops and a gay best friend on my arm. With an idealistic, fairytale notion ingrained somewhere beneath bleached blonde hair, I rang his doorbell with a white, French-tipped fingernail. He swung the door open, wearing a shirt that said "Killer" in brown boldface type across the chest. A part of me knew then that I was buying a ticket for a turbulent ride, but after one shared glance with my friend, I stepped across the cracked concrete to the land of marble where I believed a dazzling life story waited...

SPRING 2009

Coming from a small town with a population of two thousand, I had moved to Tyler, Texas, with the notion of it being a city. I unpacked boxes and put away dishes with thoughts of a new life in a town with its very own shopping mall. And a Walgreens. *How could a girl get so lucky?*

I'd graduated in the top ten of my high school class, and my grades would've taken me anywhere, but I told people that I chose UT Tyler because they "offered the most scholarship money." While that nugget held truth, the full truth was I didn't want to move away from my high school love.

Once I was in Tyler, the newness of the town and my high school romance faded like the image on a dilapidated postcard. It became just a picture of a place I'd once traveled to, from the fridge to the junk drawer, and left me itching to explore the world outside of a town with a population of 100,000. Was this how life worked? Did we move from one excitement to the next, in hopes or in search of some sort of fulfill-ment to quiet a deeper dissatisfaction? Or was that just me?

Tyler, known as the Rose City, was the town where you drove to the county line for booze and consistently ran into your exes. You couldn't help but date your friends' exes because the dating pool within city lim-its was rather narrow. Unless...unless you were an *opportunist* with an adventurous spirit and found an older man from Dallas to sponsor a life-experience fund.

During freshman year in 2006, while lounging on the couch between classes, I came across an episode of *Dr. Phil*. The show featured a pretty, young girl and an older gentleman discussing their story of love after meeting on a specific online dating website—*sugardaddyforme.com*. He filled the age gap with lavish gifts, money, trips, and condos. I held a natural affinity for older men as they were more experienced, had more stories to tell, and were more mature...or so I believed at the time. The show was meant to be cautionary, but back then, I ran straight to any-thing that promised a good time and story. The warning added to the thrill and reassured my growing inferiority complex that I could live life differently, more exceptionally, than most.

Retrieving the dented laptop from my room, I completed the regis-tration process in less than twenty minutes. I was five-foot-eleven, and my legs dangled off the end of my twin-sized bed. While I longed for an upgrade, I don't think it dawned on me just where else the men on this site would want those legs to dangle.

Ping. Ping. Ping. The inbox of my new online profile exploded. Even if I never met any of these guys, I loved the attention as I skimmed through some of the messages. *What the hell is a cuckold?* I scanned the space for my roommate before googling the answer.

I shut the laptop with wide eyes.

Yet curiosity lingered later that evening while browsing the site of private jets and pretenders with my bulging eyes. After email exchanges with married men and men with fetishes that freaked me out more than they turned me on, I deleted my profile.

But three years later, on the day I blew out twenty-one candles on my birthday cake, I couldn't wait for adventure any longer. So, I created another profile, but this time I had a little more determination and a lot more alcohol in my system.

One Thursday afternoon while sitting in World Geography, my BlackBerry vibrated. When the professor turned his back on the room to write on the dry erase board, I read a text message from a man on the sugar daddy dating website. His profile spouted witty, entertaining comments and indicated he had never been married nor had any children. Photos of him running the bulls in Pamplona and skiing the slopes in Colorado charged my interest. Unless I was being catfished, he was a tall, blue-eyed forty-seven-year-old man with a wide smile. He displayed photos from across the world with captions that appealed to my love of indulgence, like, *"Can't choose between the beach or the snow? You don't have to—I have homes in both."*

"Let's get drunk and make questionable decisions?" Bradley's text said.

Glancing at the atlas on my desk, I fiddled the corner pages of the book with my fingers. I longed to see the world from that book spring to life, to immerse myself in places, to understand people without speaking the same language, to have a story to tell.

The semester was almost over. *Fuck it.*

"Okay, I'm in," I typed.

When my friend and I drove through the guard gate of his Preston

Hollow subdivision that next weekend, my mouth dropped in awe at the massive homes. Trees lined the streets. The large homes, spaced at least an acre apart, displayed manicured and landscaped lawns. Vibrant flowers and decadent bushes were symmetrically interspersed across the yards. I'd never been close to so much opulence. I'm not sure I had known it really existed then, and I felt a bit like a Beverly Hills Hillbilly, having grown up push-mowing the lawn in a bikini to get a workout and a tan all in one swoop...ya know, efficiency. Didn't seem like I could do that here.

I was freakishly nervous about meeting someone from the sugar daddy website. Although it was 2009 and the internet was becoming more like the local coffee shop, this was pre-app-swiping era and my first experience meeting someone from the web. My friend, Colin, provided emotional support, but he could've also doubled as a witness.

Bradley opened the door and stepped back in surprise.

"Oh my," he said. "Come in."

Shifting his weight between his legs and surveying us, an awkward silence passed before he said, "Just smoked a joint...Y'all want a tour?"

My head bounced around like a bobblehead doll as I told myself, *act cool, act natural,* but my nerves had already dried my tongue and attached it to the roof of my mouth.

He guided us up the winding staircase. Gripping the black handrail, I became hyper-aware of my physical movements. I placed one foot in front of the other and glanced in a hallway mirror, never imagining the endless evenings to come when Bradley and I would snort Scarface-style cocaine rails off them until sunrise. Colorful art from around the world highlighted the walls, hinting at future experiences that I could already taste. At the top of the steps, a large, provocative photograph of a brunette woman hung mounted on the wall. Her hands wrapped behind her head and her confident gaze screamed, Come fuck me. Who was she, and was he looking for that same sexual prowess in me?

Stepping into his home office, the rows and rows of books, photos, and certificates impressed me.

"What did you study?" I asked.

"Philosophy," he said.

After settling into the chairs in front of his large desk, we bonded over us all being from small towns before he said, "So, I know you want to date someone with money."

Surprised, I nodded a timid admittance, jarred by his blunt directness.

"How 'bout a little birthday shopping at Neiman's?"

Colin and I glanced at one another. I had never set foot inside a Neiman Marcus store. The closest I'd gotten was the clearance shoe rack at Dillard's. Fashion was designer jeans and a cute tank top.

"Sure," I said.

He called his driver and minutes later, we had piled into the back of a black Cadillac Escalade and were being dropped off at the North Park mall entrance of Neiman's.

I perused jewelry at the David Yurman counter before Bradley tapped on the glass.

"That one," he said to the saleswoman.

He's buying me jewelry? Winner, winner. Wait, do I owe him something in return?

We hadn't outlined the parameters of any relationship or arrangement. An arrangement, according to one sugar website, was "where people are direct with one another and stop wasting time. It allows people to immediately define what they need and want in a relationship." I wanted adventure, but I'd discover as soon as I slept with him that I'd be wanting him to be my Prince Charming too. I lacked in the direct communication department and continued to try and get a read for what he wanted, never stopping to just, I don't know, ask.

His personal shopper approached us as the woman placed the thick silver and amethyst cable bracelet on my wrist. I changed into a fitted ruffled gray dress and multicolored Tod sandals the shopper selected. While in the dressing room, I turned the bottom of the sandal over and was shocked over the price. *$350? For a sandal?* I lived with Colin at the time, and my portion of the rent cost the same. I didn't spend $350 on books for a semester or on groceries for a month.

When I stepped out of the dressing room, Bradley nodded his approval, and I tossed my wrinkled clothes into a silver bag. Bradley picked out a pair of Prada slip-on loafers for Colin before we headed to a local sports bar.

Offsetting the glamour of Neiman's, we traipsed into 1st & 10, a dimly lit sports bar appealing to spectators with its no-frills grime. Sports announcers broadcasted on the large televisions mounted to the far wall. Within minutes and without stopping to ask him, the waitress placed a Crown & Coke in front of Bradley.

"Same drink since the fourth grade," he said.

His boisterous personality relieved some of the pressure to make small talk. I didn't want to say anything wrong. Awed by the amount of money he'd just spent on me, I wanted him to like me and leaned into his body. I giggled and ran my fingers through my hair, primping like a peacock.

We lifted our drinks in the air and clinked glasses.

"Cheers," I said.

I washed down rounds and rounds of vodka sodas, an attempt to chug the nerves away.

After the dingy sports bar, his driver dropped us off at a strip club, Million Dollar Saloon. Allured by the darkness, the grit, and the pounding bass, I enjoyed the strip club as well.

Women of all shapes and colors dotted the multiple stages and spun around the slender poles. I admired the dancers, how tuned into their sexuality and bodies they seemed. While I'd had a drunken go at a local amateur night the year prior, I often slumped my shoulders to blend in with a crowd, lacking confidence in my own body. They were tapped into a power I hadn't embodied, and I didn't know how to honor my sensuality then.

I admired their beautiful feminine forms because, while I hadn't spoken my truth with anyone at the time, I had always been sexually drawn to women as well as men. I chalked up any of my encounters with women as being a liquor lesbian.

A security guard led us to the VIP balcony area. Red lights shimmered across the dancer's G-strings and body glitter. I sat in one of the comfortable, suede chairs next to Bradley. Bradley bought a lap dance for Colin, who laughed off the exotic female grinding. Watching his arms fling about awkwardly was quite humorous, as he didn't know what to do with his hands or what to do with the naked woman in front of him.

Back at Bradley's house for a little cocaine to balance all of the drinking, Colin and an attorney friend of Bradley's played pinball upstairs while Bradley grabbed me by the hand to lead me to his room. My heart raced, feeling like the quarterback had just chosen dorky me.

We took the steps two at a time, passing the Pamplona bull mural next to his master suite. He laid me down on the king-sized bed, pulled the new dress down to reveal my naked breasts, and used his black American Express to sprinkle the white powder on one before he leaned down to inhale and lick around my nipple.

Although I assumed sex was part of our equation, I hadn't planned on sleeping with him that first night. The liquor decreased my ability to play hard to get, and I relinquished myself to the carnal temptation. He spread my tense, tight thighs, gave his penis a pep talk and a couple of encouraging pep taps, and entered me. I turned my face to the side, checked out, and didn't make eye contact with him.

I wasn't very experienced then, but I now know I held sexual traumas from losing my virginity. At twelve, I'd snuck off to an older boyfriend's house with intentions of losing ours to one another, but at the last minute, I had changed my mind. When I voiced my no, the boyfriend pressured me until the no became a yes. The physical pain wasn't the only thing that lingered from that evening. The discarding of my feelings conditioned me to acquiescence to a man's superior need.

While Bradley and I were having sex, he abruptly pushed himself off. I felt an urge to do something, an ancestral hunger to appease him, but I didn't know what. The walls closed in around me as I laid rejected and unsure how to redeem myself. He'd outed me as the sexual fraud.

"You're the most beautiful yet most boring lay of my life," he yelled, stomping into the adjoining bathroom.

What had I done wrong? But, most beautiful? Compared to the woman on his wall, I measured up? Did he really think I was the most beautiful?

It's interesting that in that moment and so many more in my life, I tended to cling onto the positive thread in the situation instead of how awful his actions were or an in-depth examination of the truth. A lover should never make one feel shame, but my self-worth expected nothing more.

The weight of the previous evening's decisions hit the next morning, radiating anxiety from my head to heart, crawling in and around every vertebra. Colin and I called in to work claiming a car battery issue prevented us from making the brunch shift at the same Tex-Mex restaurant, and when we got home, I remember feeling as if I were showering the shame away.

A week had passed when my phone vibrated on a lunch shift. I pulled the device out of the black apron tied over my black pants.

"Sat you a three top. Businessmen," Colin said with a wink when he passed me in the kitchen, pausing to flirt with our dishwasher, a Mexican man who nodded and wiped the white plates clean with a dirty dishrag.

"Thanks," I said and looked back down at my phone.

I double-checked the name when I saw the message displayed *Bradley*. He had thrown himself off of me so fast that I was surprised he'd reach out ever again. *Maybe he didn't remember?* I leaned against the painted cinder block wall to read the text.

"*Come to Mexico with me? We can leave on Wednesday and return whenever we want. Bring Colin or whoever you'd like,*" he stated, as if everything in my world revolved around a schedule based on his desires.

I tapped my fingers to the beat of the Latin music from an overhead speaker while I considered my response.

"Gringa, I'm not recooking these enchiladas," Carlos, the cook, said as he gestured to a plate of food waiting to be served under the heat lamp.

"Sí, sí, ese."

I shoved the phone back into my server's apron and picked up the plate with a small, square oven mitt. Bradley must've liked something about me. I chalked his shouting up as a one-time drunken outburst and focused on his positive attributes. His humor and how he reminded me of Pearl Jam's Eddie Vedder. How his charisma charmed me and how his intelligence both intimidated me and turned me on. *Would I be crazy to go to Mexico with a man I've barely known a week?*

Exhausted after a busy shift of running around, I unhooked my bra as soon I walked through the front door of our townhouse apartment, my breasts and myself free of being held together for the public. I flung the bra into my room, providing an instant release and comfort that I loved in many aspects of my life.

"Colin...Colin!!"

"What?"

He stood shirtless in our shared bathroom, looking in the mirror and meticulously piecing his spiked, bleach blond hair strand by strand. Perching on the closed toilet seat next to him, I asked, "Wanna go to Mexico?"

"Shut the hell up. You bitch. Commas aren't in the right places in my bank account right now. Or any commas at all, for that matter."

"Speaking of, you owe me for rent," I said.

"I'll give it to you tomorrow. Back to Mexico, slut. Give me the deets."

"I'm dead serious. Bradley offered to take us both. You have a passport, right?"

Colin was the person I went to when I needed an extra little nudge for anything risqué. I'd known him since he played The Boy and I played Dixie Wicks in a Mt. Vernon Junior High play, *Once Upon a Playground*—when he and I were both "straight." I'd known him long enough to know he'd give me just the right amount of confidence to go on this trip.

With school out for the summer, I reserved those long, hot days for a strict sleep and drink regimen, minus the waitressing shifts. A couple of years prior, while considering marrying a Costa Rican friend for him to obtain a green card, I had applied for my passport as a "just in case." This mere mention of an escape perked my energy, an opportunity to travel outside of the country for the first time. I craved life experiences with an insatiable intensity. Each new adventure offered a fleeting satisfaction, as if I were an addict who had a hold on the dragon, even if only for a moment. I longed to live some of the stories I'd read, to learn, and to find the inspiration to move my pen. Travel seemed to be the best, maybe only, way to live a full life, and I planned to gorge myself on experiences.

The smell of saltwater permeated my mind with a daydream of basking in the Yucatan sunshine. What did I have to lose, the waitress job I'd held for a record four months? I could always find another one. I pushed the fact that I had only known Bradley for a week out of my head. What was the worst that could happen?

"We're in," I responded to Bradley. *"Ready for some fun in the sun!"*

Colin and I jumped up and down, chanting, "We're going to Mexico, we're going to Mexico."

And with that one decision, for better or worse, I altered the course of my life. I'd come to receive an abundance of lavish experiences, money, and opportunities. I'd be presented with an assortment of gifts. Two of those being heartbreak and a deep-running sense of unfulfillment.

With only two days until departure, we hustled to get our shifts covered. Our coworkers questioned how we were both traveling to Mexico on a sudden whim. We made up a lie about a rich uncle since having a sugar daddy seemed a bit taboo for acquaintances or coworkers. I blared music while we packed and sang into our hairbrushes. We spun around in our undies, throwing clothes and swimsuits into our suitcases.

When we drove through the gate at the private airport in Addison, *Million Air*, Bradley joked, "My baby doesn't ride coach. She wears it."

Passing the open airplane hangar, I walked to the tarmac where the Citation V awaited. As we boarded the plane, I felt as if my childhood fantasy of being a famous actress had been actualized. Each step felt more and more glamorous, like stepping into a life I was born to lead. I welcomed the indulgence and the extravagance, the leisure of a plane departing when we wanted it to, the jet setting to the Riviera Maya. Yet a part of me also felt like an imposter. Who was I to lead such a lavish life? Did having nothing growing up entitle me to the life of my dreams?

Bradley climbed into the plane and plopped a bag of McDonald's on an open seat—ironic because only three days prior I had less than $100 in my bank account. Without his invitation, the dollar menu would have likely been one of my only food options for the next two weeks.

After a turbulent flight that left me expecting death, I placed my hand above my eyebrows to shield the sun as we deplaned and entered a bare, white-walled building. I had prepared myself to enter a long customs line, but to my delight, the private airport had no such thing.

Colin and I locked eyes with a smirk. Without exchanging any words, I knew he was experiencing the same happy dance on the inside—the *are you kidding me, is this happening* type of dance. We each pressed a button to proceed out of customs, green-lit from having our bags searched.

After an hour and a half on the road, we arrived at my dream Spanish-style house, Casa Luna, a private oceanside villa in Akumal.

Astonished by the detail as we walked about the sprawling mansion, I consciously kept my jaw from dropping and exchanged glances with Colin. *Is this real?* Dark blue tiles rimmed the outer edge of the pool and etched an L in the center. Hand-carved mahogany and antiques furnished each of the seven bedrooms. The in-room bathrooms were adorned with colorful, hand-painted tiles and marble. Jokingly, I thought, *That's it, Bradley is going to have to get me pregnant.*

I was the same little girl who experienced joy over pressing hotel elevator buttons over and over. Walking around Casa Luna carried the same excited feeling. Containing the giddiness proved rather difficult, and I felt an inexplicable urge to rein in my joy, to act cool. The little girl inside cartwheeled, delighted in the wonder and awe of new experiences. Yet I muffled the grin threatening to expose how I felt out of place. It was as if I were experiencing two simultaneous moments...the one I was allowed to have and the one I hid. The one I assumed others anticipated and the raw, unfiltered one.

Bradley and I stayed up late that evening for cocktails and conversation. His eyes lit up as he told stories in what I'd later determine was his manic state.

"We need Mexico names," he said. "I'm Alejandro Caliente." He tilted his head to the side before exclaiming, "Kristina! You're Kristina."

Kristina remained my alias for the trip and the majority of our seven-year relationship. For a time, blaming my poor decisions on an alternate personality separated those choices from my responsibility. Those decisions were made as another person, apart from me. Years later, I'd have to sift through her actions to get to the core of me.

"Come on, Kristina, let's go to the roof," he said.

He grabbed my hand and led me up three flights of stairs to the rooftop terrace. Stars dotted the expansive sky. The ocean water splashed against the rocks below. *Alejandro Caliente* climbed upon the ledge of the roof and yelled, "Name a Shakespearean play."

"*Romeo and Juliet*," I said.

These violent delights have violent ends
And in their triumph die, like fire and powder,
Which, as they kiss, consume.

His hands dramatically flung about, expressing his love for the literature as he recited it, word for word.

"*Midsummer Night's Dream.*"

Love looks not with the eyes, but with the mind,
And therefore is winged Cupid painted blind.

"*Hamlet.*"

Doubt thou the stars are fire;
Doubt that the sun doth move;
Doubt truth to be a liar;
But never doubt I love.

With each recitation, I stood transfixed, gazing upwards at him with doe-eyed wonder. His energy made me feel alive—and furthered a pattern of looking to men to fulfill something I believed at the time I was missing, a need to complete me.

I fell in love with him in this picturesque moment. Looking back, I fell in love with the *idea* of him as well, for the life he could provide and the Prince Charming he could be, something I believe many girls have been culturally conditioned to believe. I yearned to deeply know this man, but I realize now I yearned to be deeply known.

While at times I might have wished I'd fallen off the ledge or to the ground, because those earthly collisions may have been less painful than the self-betrayal and the verbal abuse to come, at that moment, I fell hard for this man I barely knew.

We retreated to the master bedroom. I slipped out of my clothes and stood in front of him, naked, vulnerable, and exposed. I struggled to find body confidence, having become more self-conscious of my body after a prominent modeling agency said they'd work with me a year prior, but only if I lost two inches in my waist and hips. When I looked in the mirror, I reacted to my body in a different way than how Bradley looked at my curves. My eyes drew to the imperfections. His eyes spoke with a hunger I'd never encountered before.

"What fabulous toys you have," he said.

He cupped a breast with one hand and my vagina with the other. We kissed before he laid me across the floral comforter. Not wanting to be considered a boring lay, I made a point to switch to different sexual positions and borrowed the blowjob pointers that Colin had demonstrated on a banana before the trip. After he finished, he held me for a few minutes before rolling over to sleep.

While showering the next morning, I peered out the glass window at the ocean and shook my head in disbelief at how I was living a life I'd once imagined. This life, these extravagant experiences were happening to me...*me*? I felt so lucky. Meeting Bradley felt like my foot had found its glass slipper.

When the staff chef placed tortilla soup in front of me at dinner that evening, he said, "For Señorita Emma."

I didn't correct him. Instead, I lowered the spoon into the red broth and grasped my wine glass to drown out any indicators that pointed to anything less than the fairy tale story I'd begun to tell myself.

When the time came to venture home, airport security officials took our temperature upon exiting the country, and we boarded the plane back to reality. Before leaving to drive back to Tyler, Bradley asked for my bank account information.

"I know you're a broke college student," he said. "Let me help you."

$2,000 appeared in my checking account the next afternoon.

*"If you don't know where you've come from,
you don't know where you're going."*

—Maya Angelou

2

THE EARLY '90S

One hot afternoon while the window air conditioning unit struggled to keep the living room cool, I glanced up from my kindergarten math homework to see Wade, a neighbor and friend I loved to hate, standing in front of the screen door of my mom's dilapidated, yellow rental home in the countryside of Northeast Texas. He stood next to the peeling paint and held the door open with his foot.

"Race ya to the hay bales," Wade said.

"Still got my math lesson," I said with a shrug.

I erased a pencil scribble to show my neat calculations for the equation, striving to uphold my spot on the honor roll. Aces on my report card ensured beaming attention from my bickering parents.

I blew the home-cut bangs out of my eyes and watched Wade for a moment. As he turned around, I laid the number two pencil down before darting out the door past him into the late August heat, my only care being winning against him in one of our many Olympic-like competitions and to stand higher on the victor's podium. His feet crunched the gravel behind me, closing the gap between us as we headed toward the open pasture between our homes.

With my head start, I pumped my arms and ignored my aching lungs until I tripped over my feet. I sat there in the dirt and examined the blend of old and fresh scabs on my knees, picking at the new wound. Blood trickled down my shin and dripped into the mismatched white socks. Wade laughed and looked over his shoulder, half a football field away.

Those same scars are still on my knees, faded from years of sun but ever hinting at my roots. They remind me of where I came from. They remind me of who I was, and who I am.

I grew up in a modest, middle- to lower-class family. I never worried about whether or when my next meal would arrive, but my mom only bought brand-name Cinnamon Toast Crunch when the box was on sale and abandoned her pride to accept school supplies from the church. I wish I could recall that laughter and love ran abundantly throughout my home, but a darker aura lingered from one of my earliest childhood memories.

One evening after dinner during that kindergarten year, the raised voices of my parents drifted into my room, the same song of disagreement on money and spending habits. I tiptoed across the red, stringy carpet into the living room. My dad deflated into his faded blue recliner, staring straight ahead at the empty screen on the television.

Climbing over the arm of the La-Z-Boy, I sat on my favorite place in the world, his lap. I adored my dad, who was the source of my given nickname, Little Tommy.

"What's wrong, Daddy?"

"Ask your mom. She's the one who wants the divorce," he said.

"Divorce? What's a divorce?"

I sensed the negative inflection from his tone of voice and knew my cradle of love had somehow been robbed by this foreign word. My mom bought us a children's book on divorce to communicate the message that their split wasn't our fault, but their separation didn't fit with how life was *supposed* to be, as I'd witnessed on our Disney VHS tapes or in my friends' unbroken homes. My parents started seeing other people, and the only bright side was that we celebrated two birthdays and two Christmases.

My younger brother, Christopher, and I visited my dad every other weekend and for a month in the summer. I flittered from her nest to his nest, never settling because I'd soon be leaving again. I'd always come home to my mom with a sense of longing for my dad.

Although maybe not his choice, my dad's departure left an abandonment wound, a dread and debilitating fear that he, and then later in life, other men, would always leave me—reinforcing an underlying notion that I must not be good enough for them to stay. And as I'd later learn, this instilled a desperate need to please and prove my worth.

Soon after their divorce, I packed a bag and started sleeping on top of my California Raisin bedspread, fearing a fire would rip my home away at any moment. Worry also consumed me, particularly about my dad's health. Anxious thoughts swarmed my young mind—what if my dad had a heart attack while he was driving for work?

On one of the visits to my dad, I rode shotgun with him in his eighteen-wheeler truck. I loved sitting high up on the road to pick up and drop loads of steel pipe for the oil field, feeling like a big girl since I was allowed to travel with him and Christopher wasn't. Riding with my dad while he worked wasn't necessarily unusual, but it made me feel special. An unspoken understanding of love rested between us. I didn't realize until much later that I yearned for that understanding to be spoken.

He lit a Marlboro Red cigarette and blew the smoke out the window. Acting as if the smoke appalled me, I leaned closer to the passenger door, rolled down the window, and blew a cough outside.

"When ya gonna stop smokin', Daddy? Ya know it's not good for you."

"I know, kiddo. But I've been smoking since I was fourteen. Easier said than done. Better you just never start," he said.

"Teacher says secondhand smoke isn't good for me either."

"Wanna play on the CB?" he asked.

He knew I loved talking to the other truck drivers on the CB radio.

"What should I say?" I asked him.

"Ask if there are any bears on the highway," he said.

"Breaker, breaker, 1-9. Any bears out there on the road?" I said, pressing the side button while glancing back at my dad. Lifting my thumb, "What are bears?"

The cigarette dangled from his thick lips as he smiled, shifted gears, and said, "Cops."

"Copy that, partner. Bear on I-30 Eastbound before Texarkana. None on Hwy 259," said a trucker.

I loved how we could communicate to the other drivers on this device, but one trucker made a crude comment about my voice that urged my dad to make a quick, snarky reply and snap the CB radio off. Something to the tune of, "That's my daughter, asshole."

"Tell me the Bronco story?" I asked.

"Well," he said, "the first and only brand-new car I ever bought was a Ford Bronco."

"And?"

"It was 1988."

"And?"

"Oooh yeah, got a baby too. Baby and a Bronco all in one year. Sure was a good year."

"I'm not a baby anymore." I said, "I'm a big girl now."

The desolate stretches of Texas highway between oil field stops seemed endless. I didn't comprehend at the time why I hid in the sleeper cabin while he unloaded the pipe at the job site, but I wasn't supposed to be riding with him at my age. Like my father, being a rebel thrilled me, doing something I wasn't *supposed* to do, flirting with danger or disobeying rules and restrictions, and living life with a little edge.

"Are we there yet? I needa pee," I said.

"What the bucket is for," he said, not looking up from jotting a time down on one of the many worn logbooks he'd stashed beneath the driver's seat. The different logbooks indicated driving breaks and stops—only he knew which book to pull in case he was pulled over and inspected by a state trooper.

"The bucket?!"

I wrinkled my nose, appalled by the yellow five-gallon bucket that I smelled before I saw. Sitting my butt over the rim, I was afraid I might fall in, but I'd already undone the top button of my Jordache jeans to relieve my bladder. After shimmying my pants down to my ankles, I hovered over the bucket and peed, grossed out when some of the contents splashed back on me.

"TP?" I asked.

"Here," he said.

His tan hand reached through the sleeper cabin's curtain to offer the one-ply tissue. I dropped the paper into the bucket and sat back in the front passenger seat, legs hovering above the red and black Peterbilt floor mats.

"How much longer till we get home?"

"Couple hours, sweetie," he said.

"Well, why ain't we goin' on the main highway?" I asked.

He lifted his arm to gesture to the world around him and said, "This is the scenic route. Best way to get somewhere ain't always the quickest."

I figured the route had something to do with the bears and kicked my legs up and down.

"Daddy, why don't you get back with Mama?"

"I've tried, Kristin," he said.

I stopped kicking my legs as the news and disappointment set in. I never doubted that my dad loved me. I sensed his love in the way he looked at me, but I longed for him to tell me he loved me more than all the stars in the sky or more than all the kernels of sand. I longed to know him on a deeper level, to know all of his stories. His father, my grandfather, had been murdered when my dad was only fourteen. I understand now that as a defense mechanism for pain, he enclosed his tenderness in a wall of silent strength. Children often carry similar wounds as their parents.

My dad made up for any disappointment by taking Christopher and me for a fun-filled weekend of McDonald's and monster truck races. When he drove us to my mom's house a couple of hours past their agreed-upon time, she stood waiting in the front yard with her arms crossed.

"Don't bring them home late again, Tommy," she yelled. "I've had enough."

She pointed her index finger into his chest. He grabbed her wrist and pushed her back.

"Don't ever point your finger at me," he said.

"Go inside," my mom said to my brother and me.

But having already witnessed the unsettling scene, I didn't understand how the two people I loved the most couldn't love one another. The fight in the front yard and the hurt in my father's eyes when he told me she wouldn't take him back shattered my hope of the cookie-cutter family ideal. Years later, I'd discover children often carry similar behaviors as their parents, too.

"It's on the strength of observation and reflection that one finds a way."

—Claude Monet

3

A couple years later, summer faded into fall and giddiness overwhelmed me as I waited at the end of the driveway for the yellow school bus. Fourth grade meant the transfer to a larger school, away from elementary school and my reputation as the "rat nest" hair girl, a result of an ill-fated decision to allow one of my mother's friends to give me a perm. I don't think giving a third grader a perm is ever a fantastic idea, but at least I'd graduated from the kitchen haircuts and raising my eyebrows to meet chunky, uneven bangs. Couple the school transfer with my new shoes, and I'd finally be one of the cool kids.

I shuffled my feet back and forth, sliding the new basketball shoes across the dirt, but carefully enough not to swirl the dust and ruin the sneakers before showcasing them to my friend and Little Dribblers teammate, Megan. When Mr. Bowen opened the bus door, I picked up my backpack and leaped up the steps.

I tapped my foot against the cracked black seat in front of me only to hop positions and rest my butt on my feet. The bus inched closer to Megan's stop at the trailer park, winding around the curvy two-lane road, only to pause at the railroad tracks. When Mr. Bowen pulled the bus up to her stop, she bounded on board and took a seat across the aisle.

"Hey, Megan! Check out these PF Flyers!" I turned my leg sideways to display the new white and blue kicks in their full wonder.

"PF Flyers? Seriously? Check out my Nikes," she said.

Her laughter echoed in the aisle, seemingly bouncing off my rejection in slow motion. The sun shimmered brighter on those black and white swooshes. I glanced at the older high school kids sitting at the back of the bus. *Had they seen? Had they heard?* Shrinking back, I wished my seat would swallow me, take me away from the mortification of being less than and not knowing what to say. I'd only wanted to be her equal, to be liked, and to be accepted. Now I only wanted to lie on the floor underneath the worn seats.

When the bus dropped me at home, I sprinted up the long driveway to await the arrival of my mom. Since she could only afford after-school daycare for Christopher, I sat alone with nothing on my mind but those Nikes.

In an attempt to pick up one of three channels, I wiggled the metal bunny ears perched on top of the TV. Frustrated by the scrambled images, I scoured the kitchen for a snack. I opened the cupboard but found my mom's disappointing diet food: canned vegetables, peanut butter, and rice cakes. I opened and closed the fridge, turning my nose up at the celery.

I tossed in a load of laundry. When the water rushed into the drum, I opened the lid of the washing machine and watched the machine come to a stop. I closed the lid and listened while the machine whirred itself to life. I opened the top again, and just as my Chicago Bulls basketball jersey, white underwear, and grass-stained shorts were coming to a halt, placed my pinky in the little latch hole to trick the machine into thinking the lid was closed. Innately curious, I enjoyed seeing the inner workings of something typically not accessible and was proud of my self-sufficiency.

When the microwave clock ticked to 5:30 p.m., my mom's blue Chevy Astro van bounced down the driveway with dust trailing behind the tires. As soon as her briefcase and pager touched the kitchen counter, I pounced.

"Maaaaaaammmaaa! We need to go to Walmart. I'm not going to survive fourth grade unless we go tonight."

"Kristin Nell, I haven't even made supper. Your room still look like a tornada hit it?"

"But that's not fair..."

"Fair is what comes to town once a year," she said.

My voice wavered. I cried and relayed the day's humiliation. "All the kids have Nikes. I don't want to go back to school."

On the drive into town, my mom introduced my brother and me to an imagination game. The game passed time on the road and allowed me to live in my future, in my hope.

"This is called Dreaming Big," she said. "There are no limits during these sessions. You can be, do, have anything you want. Now, who wants to go first?"

"Me, me, me," I said, leaning forward from the back seat.

"Sit back and buckle up, or ya want a whippin' when we get home?"

"She can go. I like listening," Christopher said.

"Okay, I'm a movie star," I said, "And live in a two-story home. There's a pool on the inside. And a theater. Cabinets full of my favorite Little Debbie snacks. Star crunches and nutty buddies. And *no* bedtime."

My mom asked as she pulled into the parking lot, "And what's your latest movie?"

"A western. I ride horses and arrest the bad guys."

I zipped out of my seat and slid open the van door with force, sprinting into the store.

"Kristin!" my mom yelled, as she shut the sliding door behind me.

Running straight to the shoe department, I scanned the display shoes for the swoosh I'd seen on the bus. An elderly woman in a blue vest stood on a short step ladder, stocking and straightening items on a top shelf.

"Ma'am, where are Nikes at?" I asked.

"Oh honey, we don't sell those 'round here," she said.

"Thought Wally World had everything!" I said.

My mom caught up, holding Christopher's hand while she stood next to me. Minutes later, we crossed the parking lot to check Payless Shoe Source, with no luck.

"I can't go back to school," I said.

"If you can just wait till the weekend, we'll drive to a store and find them," she said.

"Gonna be sick till the weekend then!"

"I don't think so, young lady."

Defeat set in.

"Hey, how about we go to Braum's for ice cream?"

After we returned home, my mom pulled the covers around me to tuck me into bed and ran her slender hand through my hair. She bent to kiss my forehead.

"Mama, did ya lock all the doors and windows?" I asked.

"Yes dear," she said.

"Didja double-check?"

"Yes," she said.

She crossed the room to flip the light switch before our nightly bouncing sentiments.

"Good night," I said.

"Goodnight," she said, "I love you."

"Love you," I said. "See you in the morning."

"See you in the morning," she said.

Soon after, my mom began attending night classes to learn how to use a computer and advanced to a supervisor position with what was then called the *Texas Department of Mental Health and Mental Retardation*. Upon receiving this new leadership role, she offered Christopher and me the choice to stay in the same town or to move one over where she'd be closer to her new job and where we'd enroll in a new school.

Life in Mt. Vernon would be smaller and cozier. But most importantly at that time, Mt. Vernon offered a clean slate. I could be anyone and lose anything undesired, like a reputation for rat nest hair. So, in the fifth grade, I walked into the new intermediate school hallway to a stride of, *I can be whoever I want to be.* Craving popularity, what I thought meant to be loved then, I morphed into an extrovert and embellished stories at lunchtime, modifying another part of myself to be accepted by others.

After a year or so of living in Mt. Vernon, my mom introduced us to a man she'd been dating. She'd carted my brother and me to the meetings, and although I'd spent most of my time spinning around outside on the tarnished merry-go-round, I recognized his face from the local

Alcoholics Anonymous building where she was earning somewhat of a PhD in Al-Anon philosophy, a support group created for people worried about someone with a drinking problem. The curly-haired gentleman in front of me appeared brighter than the morose man I had seen staring into a chipped coffee mug, who only looked up to ash his cigarette.

"I'm Lonnie," he said as he offered his hand, beaming from ear to ear.

I shook his hand with a bit of trepidation but made sure to wrap my small hand around his for a firm squeeze.

Lonnie moved into our new brick home, and after a few months, in the spring of 2000, they sat Christopher and me down at our wooden kitchen table with dinner from Dairy Queen resting in the center.

I ripped through the chicken finger basket as I observed my mom and Lonnie together, dipping a couple of skinny french fries in ketchup and white gravy. The cream of the gravy combined with the ketchup to make a delicious salty and sweet combination, the best of both worlds. My plastic red spoon broke off into the Butterfinger Blizzard. I brought the short shard of the spoon to my lips, licked it clean, and raised my eyebrows. They looked at one another.

"Your mom and I have decided to elope," said Lonnie.

I hope he doesn't think he can tell me what to do.

Defiance built inside and erupted with allegiance to my dad. But for the first time, I witnessed a respectful and tender relationship, with their only argument consisting of who would call the other honey bunches or bunches of honey.

Lonnie provided a strong base for support, both emotional and financial. They used my mom's income to pay off their combined debt, and despite her continuing to work and later becoming a board member of MHMR, I initially recalled his arrival into our lives as how a man helped save a woman. Despite my mom not wanting nor needing to be saved, I borrowed the notion from the fairy tale love stories I consumed as a child and discarded my mom's tenacity and drive, not recognizing that she was the one who had instilled those same traits in me until now. I'd learn that my dad had split the cost of braces and glasses with Lonnie and my mom, but I remember thinking then that with the arrival of this new man and his income, my teeth were straightened, and my eyes were enhanced—seemingly with a wave of his magic money wand.

One day after I'd poked the clear contacts into my eyeballs, I screamed at my reflection in the mirror. Lonnie and mom rushed to the edge of my bathroom door.

"This is what I really look like?" I whined, pinching at my hip bone.

Lonnie laughed, "You'd look beautiful in no makeup and a toe sack."

"Toe sack?"

"A burlap potato sack," he said.

I held every word he'd said under immediate scrutiny, thinking he only wanted to win me over. Until about a year later, around the time I was twelve, when our relationship deepened after a junior high track meet.

A drop of sweat fell from my nose to my lips. I tasted the salt and wiped the sweat off my palms on my purple and white athletic shorts. Nerves pinballed around in my stomach, and I hoped I wouldn't catch a case of nervous pooping. I dug the spikes into the red, squishy track and crouched to set my position, glancing over my right shoulder at a competitor.

"Runners. On your mark," the announcer said.

I hiked my butt into the air and took off at the sound of the starting pistol. I sped down the second lane and cleared each hurdle until crossing the 100-meter finish line. I folded over, placed my hands on my knees, and panted before walking off the track with my fingers interwoven behind my head. As I scanned for a familiar face in the crowd, Lonnie stood and waved from the silver bleachers. Everything in me wanted to not like him, but he kept showing up for me. I changed into sandals before meeting him on the steps.

"You looked like a little deer out there," he said. "Bounding over those hurdles."

"Thanks. I think. Anyway, that was my last event," I said.

He tossed me the keys to his green single-cab Chevy pickup truck.

"Why don't you drive us home?" he asked.

"I don't know how to drive a standard," I said, tossing the keys back.

"I'll pull over into the empty parking lot and show you."

We spent the next hour driving in that deserted lot, him teaching me how to drive the manual transmission. Controlling the shifting gears, I loved feeling in charge of the revved engine.

"Pause at the top of that little hill," he said.

Met with the incline and gravitational force, the truck rolled backward.

"Lonnie! I can't do this," I exclaimed, jumping the vehicle to a stop.

"Patience, Little Deer. Yes, you can. Press your left foot on the clutch and your right foot on the gas. Gently press the gas and at the same time, release the left foot slowly."

After a couple of sputtered attempts, I found the sweet spot of acceleration, shifted, and left the parking lot empowered with a new belief in my capability.

Despite my initial resistance, Lonnie became a man I admired and one I went to for advice, valuing his non-mainstream, brave opinions. Laying a printed copy next to him, I shared an essay on change and divorce that I planned to publish as the editor for the new school newspaper. He'd nudged me to start the newspaper, *The Tiger's Growl*, with another class-mate when I'd complained about not having a junior high newspaper. In the article, I spoke about how change is the only constant in life, offered counsel to my classmates, and shared my experience of divorce.

"You have a way with words, Little Deer. I wouldn't be surprised if you do something with the gift someday. Listen...I want you to ask yourself a question. Take money out of the equation; what do you want to do with your life? What do *you* want to do?"

He asked with an implied knowing that I could accomplish any-thing I wanted, free of any doubts or backup plans. My mind jumped to how I'd always been a fiend for stories; whether begging my mom to tell one more from her childhood—of eating squirrel brains, using an outhouse, or accidentally mooning her entire high school class—or devouring books, my thirst for stories remained unsatiated.

I loved watching movies and reading. I escaped to the pages of Nancy Drew and Mary Higgins Clark, went back in time with Laura Ingalls Wilder. I'd envision myself as the main character, experiencing all of the wonderful adventures and solving the mysteries, playing the author's words like a movie in my mind. I loved telling stories and I longed to live a good story. I connected to the characters in books as if they were my friends. The stories made sense when my life didn't. They presented a big world of possibility outside the confines of a small town and incited my craving for adventure and experiences as I knew they'd become my stories to tell.

"No limits? I'd tell stories. Write. Act. Yeah, storytelling," I said and nodded my head.

"Then do it. Life is closer to your imagination than you think. Follow your passion, and you'll never work. The money will naturally come."

That same year, inspired by the new guru in my home, I wrote a screenplay with one of my closest friends, Kristen. After passing a spiral notebook back and forth, we typed it up on the computer and Lonnie saved our work on a floppy disk. I still have the disk we saved *The Miracle of a Tragedy* on, which is about as good as the title suggests. But then again, who are we to judge our creativity?

Lonnie and I started a tradition of dad and daughter dates to further our discussions. We'd go to dinner and a movie, but my favorite part was on the drive to and from the theater when we'd discuss his new-age philosophy and life outlook. He treated me like an adult, like an equal, and to my teenage surprise, valued my opinion. I'd grown accustomed to people treating me younger than I'd always felt. He offered fresh ideas and endless possibilities, helping me believe in them for myself.

Living in the Bible Belt, my inner pressure to go to church conflicted with the judgment and fear experienced when a youth pastor yelled to attendees, "What if you die in a wreck on the way home tonight? Don't you want to be saved?"

The pastor's words didn't seem to be on the right side of Jesus. So, after school one day, I slung my backpack onto the couch and paused next to Lonnie, who typed with fervor at the computer in the hallway.

"Why don't we go to church anymore?" I asked.

"Little Deer, you likely believe only what you grew up around."

"What do you mean? I'm Southern Baptist."

"Look at this map of religion," he said. "See India. The Middle East. Mexico."

His finger slid across the bright, multicolored image on the monitor. The different color blocks were separated by countries, water, or larger pieces of land. If I only believed what I grew up around, how did I know what I truly believed? And if this was true for religion, what else could this be true for? How would I know what I liked if I didn't experience or research it? I reckoned that it'd be hard to stand firm behind a belief unless I explored the options.

"But...what about hell?" I asked.

"I don't believe in hell," he said.

No hell?

"If God is all-knowing and all-powerful, wouldn't they be able to design an existence without it? One could perceive time on Earth as hell. Maybe interpretations of stories morphed over time. I think we look for or see greatness as something outside of ourselves when that's not the case."

New neural pathways fired as these expansive possibilities were presented as alternatives to the information I'd accepted as truth. My mind expanded, widened with my receptivity. *What beliefs do I hold that aren't my parents'? What do I believe?*

"Well, what happens when we die?" I asked.

He laughed before continuing. "That's a good question. Everything is energy. Everything you see has a vibration. You, me, the trees, everything. Energy can't be created or destroyed; it transfers or changes from one form to another. Maybe we transfer out of this body and into a different realm or dimension."

"So, reincarnation?" I asked.

"Maybe. If you think about it, we are in the womb and then transfer to this reality, this experience. Maybe at death, we transfer to one beyond the comprehension of our five senses."

His words swirled around in my mind as I tried to make sense of the information. He worked at a power plant and said the words with such conviction, I accepted that everything was energy, although I didn't fully grasp what a *vibration* was then.

"This is a lot to take in," I said, admiring his intelligence and craving his respect.

Was my belief in something higher than myself actually mine or simply what I'd grown up around? Fear-based sermons had steered me out of the church, feeling the teachings were incongruent with my nature. I didn't realize at the time that fear itself was incongruent with our truest essence.

Lonnie fueled my curiosity with this knowledge, but the information negated everything I'd learned in a childhood of Bible School and church camps. On occasion, I joined my classmates at church since it was the cool and acceptable thing to do, but I liked the idea of life without a judgmental preacher or a damning God. That belief path felt lighter and more enjoyable.

"Life is about balance, Little Deer. You'll feel and know when you teeter one way more than the other and understand what works for you. Learn to listen to your inner guide."

An inner guide was as foreign as all of the countries he'd referenced on the religion map, but I valued and respected his insight and intelligence. On the way home from school one day, dying to pass on this information, I shared the discovery and belief with a classmate. When her face scrunched into tears instead of the look of relief I'd anticipated, I asked, "Katie, what's wrong?"

"I'm afraid you're gonna go to hell. I'm going to put you on the prayer list," she said.

Looking back, I see how this interaction shook and shrank my confidence in sharing my truths. Fearful to be rejected or condemned to hell, which felt like the same thing, I muted myself to be more agreeable for a while.

I wouldn't realize the value and importance of Lonnie implanting this information during our conversations until a couple of decades passed. I'm forever grateful for how his insight wielded my beliefs and upbringing—no matter the pain I'd come to experience or the balance I'd struggle to find.

Truth be told, I'd written about a tragedy before I'd experienced one, but I would know soon enough.

On a blistering July afternoon in 2002, I crawled out of the blue and white ski boat at my dad's house. I wrapped a towel around my waist, making sure to hide the silver belly button ring, and walked up the hill. I changed out of my bikini and hung the pieces to dry across the shower curtain rod. Droplets of water splashed against the linoleum floor as I pulled my stepmom's prosthetic leg out of the sink to brush my teeth.

I walked into the living room, passing my snoring dad on his faded blue recliner. The remote rested on his lap and he stirred when I pressed a button to mute the monotone voice of the History channel. I sat in the computer chair, clicked a couple of buttons, and heard the tune of dial-up internet. Ah, the sound of glory and connectivity!

"You've got mail," the machine said.

I signed into AOL Instant Messenger to flirt with random strangers and logged onto MSN to chat with my friends. The computer beeped and a square box appeared on the lower right-hand side of the monitor screen, indicating that Wade S. had signed on. Since Wade and I lived in separate towns, it'd been several months since we spoke or chatted. I envisioned that we'd grow up and visit a coffee shop, reminisce about the good ol' days of racing one another across the pasture or pretending we were Olympian swimmers going for the gold. *Something* told me to send him a message. To be completely honest, what we chatted about escapes my memory. But by the time I finished, my dad had awoken. Matters of religion still weighed heavy on my mind, and I sometimes cross-referenced Lonnie's knowledge with my dad's viewpoint.

"Daddy, why don't you go to church?"

"This is my church," he said as he gestured to the serene lake behind his house.

I didn't grasp what he meant as he peered at the water lapping against the shoreline, the peace offered by nature. Only now do I appreciate the healing power of spending time in nature, or that I am nature. But since my dad was less forthcoming with his reasoning, his response registered as a non-answer. I settled with myself that Lonnie might have won the round.

He grabbed the remote to scan the channels before ending up back at the History channel.

"Would you grab your dear ol' daddy a beer, sweetie?" he asked.

Grabbing beers for him was the norm. In college, my dad would tell me drinking was a slippery slope, but until then, we drove to the beer store for two thirty packs on the way to his house after he'd picked my brother and me up for the weekend.

A few days passed, and a friend of mine called.

"Wade died in a car wreck," she said.

"Not funny," I said and slammed the cordless phone back onto its receiver.

Please, don't be true. I pleaded with God, nature, Buddha, or whomever, for the news to be false. I grabbed a thick phonebook sitting on the counter and looked in the Yellow Pages for funeral homes. I slid my finger down the page and across the listings. My hand shook as I dialed the number. The pounding in my heart increased with each ring of the telephone call.

"Curry-Welborn Funeral Home," a man said.

"Hi, yes? I want to check to see if...arrangements...?"

I didn't know how to ask, didn't want to ask, for details on my friend's death, but I wouldn't believe the news until I heard it from the source. Until then, I could convince myself the news was a prank, a cruel joke.

"For Wade Stinson." My voice cracked.

"Yes. Visitation Thursday. Funeral on Friday. Sorry for your loss."

The man's news etched finality, carved the loss and pain into my being. Slamming the phone into the receiver, I retreated to my room. My whole body heaved. I'd never known a heartbreak like the loss of someone I loved until then. Over the years, I'd become so acquainted with death that loss compelled me to start looking for gifts in the grief. If I kept experiencing the heartbreaks, there must be something to learn from death. There had to be a miracle in the tragedy, a pain to gain from the loss.

Sitting next to my mom in the church for the funeral, I wrung a hand in hers, wiped the moisture from my other palm onto my dress, and looked up to the stained-glass windows as Cher's "If I Could Turn Back Time" filled the room. Guilt weighed me down as I reviewed moments I'd been mean or rude to Wade, and I pleaded for his forgiveness. As I sat in the pew, photos of Wade were projected onto a screen. I drifted to how he gave me my first kiss in between hay bales in the barn, how we chased after one another, how we raced in the swimming pool, and how we hunted for dinosaur bones in the pasture.

Destroyed over my shattered visualizations of our future, I'd assumed we'd sip coffee and reminisce about the good ol' days eventually. This first experience with death gave me only a glimpse into the disappointment brought on by expectations and assumptions, into taking life and people for granted.

When the song faded and the eulogy ended, the preacher offered the room the chance to share their sentiments. My knees wobbled and knocked on my walk to the front of the room. Fear bounced around my throat like bees and spoke discouragement. I fought through it because I wouldn't have been able to forgive myself if I didn't say something.

Unfolding a worn piece of paper behind the podium, I summoned all the strength I had to speak in front of the packed room and read a poem I'd written. Writing had become my water, and I drank to quench the pain. I don't remember all of the words, but I recall the ending.

"...help me, Wade...make me brave."

As we filed out of the church, I placed the folded, sweaty paper into the casket.

Losing him catapulted me into depressive darkness for the first time. When high school started the next month, I planned my funeral and shared the playlist with Lyndsay, my new best friend. Lyndsay wrote letters, folded pieces of notebook paper into origami, and passed the shaped notes to me between classes. She pleaded for the return of her friend, for the return of my smile. I couldn't shake the images of Wade and me, of our envisioned future from the forefront of my mind, or how much life he'd had left to live. We were supposed to live long lives together.

The initial brute force of this mortality reminder faded with time. Lyndsay started accompanying me on my weekend visits to my dad. Not wanting to amplify concern and wanting to be strong, I smiled again, not for myself, but for the worried people around me. I disliked the furrowed brows and the routine *"I'm here if you need to talk."* This set my precedent for handling loss—retreat and act like all is well. But the truth was, the loss infiltrated my mind with thoughts of suicide. Life, I'd witnessed, would pick up again after I was gone.

One night, after a few months of this darkness and an examination of my mom's medicine cabinet to remedy the pain, Wade visited in a dream. He appeared bright and happy with a big smile splayed across his face, elevated above with a glowing white and gold aura. There was a certain ethereal quality to the dream that I hadn't felt while awake, and in this one, I knew I was dreaming. My conscious mind was alert. And he was very much alive.

"Kristin," he said, "I'm okay."

"You are?" I asked.

"Yes," he said as if that was the silliest question I could've asked.

The dream lingered after I woke—the subconscious realm felt palpable and filled me with ease. I spoke with a rapid urgency when I recalled the dream to Lyndsay the next day, "But, Lyndsay, he was there!"

Doubt exuded from her body language, from the tilt of her head and the bite of her lip. I sensed she didn't know what to say nor did she want to shatter my heart again. I reconciled with myself that I didn't need her or anyone else to believe me. My heart spoke to the truth of the dream.

This was my first experience communicating with a spirit, but it would not be the last. After Wade's special visit, life became lighter, allowing me to move past the hurt and begin to heal. His death pushed me to search for my own reckoning in the world, to seek out stories and answers...even though I hadn't formed all of my questions yet.

"There is a fine line between naivety and optimism; out of goodwill, some people tend to cross that line."

—Omar Sharif

4

SUMMER 2009

A few weeks after returning home from Mexico, I woke to a craving for Taco Bueno. The intensity of it registered as odd because I rarely ate unhealthy fast food. Food existed in two categories: what would keep me skinny and what wouldn't. Taco Bueno was not in the former column. Caressing my breasts, I noticed an increased sensitivity to the point of being painful. Intuition nipped, and I pleaded with myself, *Oh no. Oh, hell, no.* Colin drove to a pharmacy to buy a home pregnancy test that I already knew the answer to.

After peeing on the stick in our bathroom, I sat for the longest three minutes of my life until the two lines confirmed my fear.

"Dude...what are you going to do?" Colin asked.

"I can't keep it, Colin."

In my mind, the cells growing inside of my body were not a baby. The cells had not advanced past being called *it*.

"I won't graduate college on time. It'd delay my life. I don't want to end up in a small town with a kid. I don't want to become one of those people who never leave."

"Whose is it?" he asked.

"Shit."

It could've been Bradley's. Or it could have been a coworker's from the restaurant. The coworker was the only younger man I'd ever slept with; yet he would not be the only one who'd go to jail or who sold drugs on the side. Not the best candidate for fatherhood. Although I loved risk-taking, there was no way I'd gamble with the slightest chance of the baby being his. Unlike many peers from my hometown, I had never dreamed of becoming a mom. The only thing I'd wanted to birth was a thrilling, adventurous life...and maybe a book. Having a baby then meant giving up everything I'd ever wanted to experience. I called Planned Parenthood and made an appointment for the following week, then called my mom and sobbed to her.

"I need you," I said.

"Are you sure you want to do this?"

"Yes," I said, "I need someone to—"

"I'll go with you," she said.

On the day before the appointment, I stayed with her so that we'd ride together. Lonnie sensed we were keeping something from him. I'd communicated how I'd started dating a wealthy man in Dallas. Lonnie and my mom knew this man took Colin and me to Mexico—they just didn't know *exactly* how we'd met. I'd told them we'd connected at a sports bar in Dallas, a version of the truth, one of several versions I'd come to love and even gravitate toward telling myself.

"Y'all meeting Bradley for lunch?" Lonnie asked, a slight edge to his voice, a squinted suspicion to his eyes.

"No," my mom insisted.

He must've sensed that we kept something from him because he stormed outside. As he paced and smoked a cigarette on the front porch, I watched him through the window. I was a bit bewildered—I'd never seen this side of Lonnie. My mom had promised not to tell anyone in the family about the abortion as most were conservative and religious. The family already considered me the weird hippy, and I didn't want Lonnie to think less of me as a person or as a daughter.

The next morning, the protesters in front of Planned Parenthood held handmade signs and wouldn't meet my eyes. In the hours between paperwork and repeated screenings, I scanned the room of women and imagined their stories, what led them to be sitting in those chairs, to have our lives intersect in such a moment. Some had men accompanying them and some did not. Eerie energy and silence hung in the air with our understanding of why each person was in the room, although nobody said anything.

"You don't have to do this, Kristin. I can help you," my mom said.

I shook my head. The entire projection of the life I wanted rested on not having the baby. During the sonogram, I turned my head, not wanting to meet my decision. Being so early on in the pregnancy, I opted to take the pill form of abortion. Taking the pill offered the easy way out, like other pills did in different aspects of my life.

The nurse instructed me to take an additional pill at home after the one in their office. Hours later, my mom tapped on the bathroom door and jiggled the handle. *Thank God I locked the knob.*

"You okay?" she asked.

I wasn't. I groaned and writhed on the cold tile floor as my body contracted. As the pangs from my belly infiltrated and penetrated my lower back, I propped myself against the cabinet and patted my sweaty forehead with a damp washcloth.

"Yes," I said through a stifled moan, not wanting to alarm her.

I've since learned that when we deny how we truly feel, we betray ourselves. But then, I believed my recklessness made me deserve every ounce of the pain.

Although the abortion was the best decision for me, shame attached its long, sticky fingers to my choice. The doctor had instructed me to not have sex for two weeks after the procedure and prescribed birth control. Bradley asked me to visit him during that time, but instead I blatantly told him about the abortion. He was shocked, yet he admired what he thought was my brutal honesty. He never knew the baby could have been his.

———————

Two months later, on a late fall evening of my senior year, I woke to a ding, opened textbooks encircling me on my bed. Without opening my eyes, I patted my hand across the white, down comforter for my phone. *"I woke from dreaming of you, angel baby. I don't want you to see other boys. Miss you."*

Bradley's words fed logs of comfort into the fire of my feeling good enough and stroked my ego with masculine reassurance. I typed a few sentiments before erasing the words; I wanted to craft the perfect, witty response. From his message, I assumed he meant that we would both only see one another.

"I'm not seeing other boys," I texted.

The next day on campus, birds flittered about as I walked along the paved pathway on the lush UT Tyler grounds. Sunlight gleamed through the windows as I sat for a Public Relations exam. I etched doodles on a scrap of paper, daydreaming, before shaking the love fog and answering questions about strategic methods for handling an organizational crisis.

Those final semesters were a delicate balance of academics and pleasure. During the week, I prioritized school. Perfectionism and people-pleasing kept me on the Dean's List. On the weekend, I transformed into a party warrior, making up for the sober streak in the middle of the week.

Most weekend evenings with Bradley started with cocktails and interspersed cocaine lines before thrilled explorations of my body. His touch carried validation, and the sounds of admiration reinforced my aspiration to do everything right. My sexual knowledge and experiences morphed from vanilla into something with a little more flavor. The erotic transformation turned me on, but my sole focus was on pleasing him.

I strived then to be like the tip of an iceberg, hiding a mystery beneath the surface. But the tip didn't connect to or originate from my truest self. The surface me began to grow more and more detached, drifting further away and melting into a person I barely recognized.

The little tomboy never envisioned herself doing lines in her undies in a rich man's bathroom, heeding his every wish. But in the moment, high on cocaine, I turned into a little marionette and did anything and everything for my puppeteer, unaware the strings would still be attached long after sunrise.

The weekend following his message, on an unusually warm mid-October evening, Bradley clumsily set up a video camera in the corner of his bedroom. His difficulties with technology illuminated the decades between us.

"Here, let me help," I said.

Helping made me useful, valuable. Pressing record, I walked into the frame, wearing nothing but a pair of his long, purple socks. Quick to follow and spout commands, he asked, "Do you want me to lick you, Kristina?"

I lowered to my knees, looked up, and nodded.

"What was that? I can't hear you. Stand against the wall and spread your cheeks," he said, tapping my face with his hand and penis.

"Yes, Master."

With eye contact forbidden, I walked to the wall, leaning into it for balance while I palmed my butt cheeks.

"What word do you want?" he asked.

"Princessa...more letters."

He licked me once and paused, waiting for my response.

"P," I said.

Anticipation built with each pause. For every lick, I spoke a letter until we completed the word.

He plugged the video recorder into a television. The bird's eye view of my body shocked me. At this new angle, my hips didn't appear fat, and I appreciated their curvaceous outline.

Around noon the next day, I opted to shower in an upstairs guest room to not wake him. Soaps, razors, toothbrushes, and facial products filled the drawers. At the time, buying twelve-dollar Venus razors made me flinch, so the stock in all of the spare bathrooms stood out. I never considered how many people traipsed in and out of his house without a full toiletry kit when I threw an extra razor or toothbrush in my bag, thrilled as if I were getting away with something.

Steam crept up the mirror as the warm water soothed my tense shoulder muscles. After stepping out of the shower and wrapping a towel around my waist, I noticed a black suitcase in the corner of the adjacent room. Tiptoeing across the white carpet to the bedroom door, I peeked at the luggage tag. Minneapolis airport. A woman's name. The date, two days before his message about not seeing other boys.

With this painful glimpse into our relationship, the air came shallow to my lungs. Hair dripping wet, I left without waking Bradley, not wanting him to see my tears and hoping my sudden absence jarred him. My mom always said that tears cleansed the soul, but these tears felt like they'd drown me. With this sting of betrayal, I vowed that I was done with Bradley.

"Why'd you leave, baby?" Bradley's text dinged five hours later while I was sitting in a psychology class.

Baby? Are you fucking kidding?

"Why tell me to stop seeing other boys if you're seeing someone else?" I texted.

"Oh, honey...I had a judgment error, but don't worry, I buried her in the backyard."

Was he drinking again already?

"Well, I sent her home coach, which is essentially the same thing."

Afterwards, he wired $3,000 into my bank account and established a precedent. Every time Bradley hurt my feelings or had a drunken outburst, money soon appeared as a peace offering. I'd turned into someone who allowed herself to be abused for money, and in the months to come, someone who'd provoke him in hopes of a financial reward.

The next time at his house, after I pillaged the other woman's suit-case for buried treasure and any clues on how to deal with this new life, I logged onto the sugar daddy website. I'd deleted my profile, but I wanted to see if Bradley's account was still active. Underneath his pic-ture, in an italicized red font, *active five hours ago* blinked. I slammed the laptop, crossed my arms, and wished shutting him out of my life was as simple as shutting the computer.

> *"Tell me, what is it you plan to do with*
> *your one wild and precious life?"*
>
> —Mary Oliver

5

A couple months after discovering Bradley dated other people, my mom visited and took me to lunch at a local diner. I'd settled into a comfortable self-inflicted drama—longing to be with him, but perplexed and indecisive whether I *should* be. Torn between the security and glamour and respecting myself, I withheld details of his infidelity when my mom asked about our relationship, fearing she'd have a negative perception of him if they met. Holding the secrets of my pain would evolve into a habit, freeing me from other people's judgments but imprisoning me in mine.

As a server restocked the sugar packets at a nearby table, my mom leaned in, her blonde hair brushing her shoulders.

"There's a spark, like I've known him for years," she said. "Like we've danced together for years. He listens. And there's something I can't put my finger on."

Bitterness boiled in my stomach, toward her and anyone who couldn't stay the course of a relationship. My mom and Lonnie had started dancing on the weekends, and at one of the places, my mom danced with another man. What started as a way to rekindle the romance now seemed to be extinguishing their ten-plus year relationship.

"I think I need to dance with him one time on my own. Just once," she said.

"And you want to stay at my apartment here...?" I asked.

"Yes. Without Lonnie."

I hated that she wanted to introduce her new man to me, to make me an accomplice in her deception. Yet how was I supposed to tell the person who'd given me everything—life, even—no? That her proposition placed me in the uncomfortable position of feeling as if I had to choose parents again, something I had felt as a teenager when given the option to choose which parent to live with. Lonnie still meant the world to me. Saying yes registered as a betrayal to me and also a betrayal to him.

I believed I was being kind to her by not voicing my true feelings then. I wanted to be an agreeable child but didn't realize my obedience was unkind toward myself and planted seeds of resentment toward her and myself. At that moment, I didn't see the good qualities she'd passed on, like kindness, intelligence, resilience, or a belief in how all things work out for a greater good. Her betrayal skewed my vision and triggered my self-hate.

I judged her and hated myself for the parts of me that were just like her. I'd adopted the dieting, the hair dyeing, the striving for male attention. We were both lost somewhere in the throes of a pretty privilege. After I recognized that my beauty emulated hers and put effort into my appearance, things in life came easier...Adoration, jobs, relationships.

The responsibility to uphold the beautiful façade for others misplaced our worth. With my value heavily placed on the surface, I'd later cross the question of whether a person even liked me beyond skin deep.

When we returned to my apartment, I went in first to clean up my messy life. I picked up a pair of yoga pants lying across the corner edge of the beige, faux-suede couch and went to the bathroom to slip them on. Makeup brushes were strewn across the countertop. I arranged the brushes into a mason jar and wiped the counter with a Clorox wipe I found underneath the sink.

My mom walked into the door, carrying a sack of groceries.

"Woo, when was the last time you did dishes?" she asked.

She started rinsing dishes and putting them into the dishwasher. I rushed to step in.

"I'll do it," I said and edged her out of the way.

The overwhelm I felt clattered like a pile of dishes collapsing into the sink. *How could I rinse my mind? And fuck, why did I have such a hard time saying no?*

My mom stood beside me, looking for an answer in my eyes. "You can say you're visiting me," I said.

A couple of months passed until that one dance with the other man led to my mom divorcing Lonnie. At the time, her leaving touched on my then-unidentified abandonment insecurities. It pained me to think of my mom abandoning Lonnie after he'd done so much for us. I felt discarded in her decision process, and the divorce touched on a similar abandonment wound held with my dad, but I affixed my attention to Lonnie's pain and unconsciously avoided addressing mine.

Although I'd come to love my mom's current partner, I didn't recognize or understand the value of choosing one's own happiness then.

While I disagreed with her actions, I admit I was envious that my mom was brave enough to act on her desire, instead of shrinking or staying to avoid discomfort, like I had chosen with Bradley.

While I'd resented my mom's philandering behavior, I'd be presented with the opportunity to evolve or resent myself. Because with a sense of humor only a divinely orchestrated Universe could have, one of the next offerings on Earth 101 placed me in a stunningly similar orbit.

*"You were a risk, a mystery, and the most
certain thing I'd ever known."*

—Beau Taplin

6

SPRING 2010

During that last year of college, time with Bradley felt like a taste of freedom at times, particularly the times when his money appeared in my account. I was excited by all the beautiful uncertainty of post-graduation life, the time that would mark the true, true start of my life. As a graduate, I'd cross into official adulthood even though part of me always felt like an older soul wrapping up experiences at Earth school.

Bradley's wire transfers covered all of my expenses, but to earn a little something of my own, I filled the time between classes during my last semester by working at a trendy clothing boutique, Heart & Soul. One April afternoon, a month or two after my mom's visit, I stood behind the register. Flipping page after page of a fashion magazine to coast through the remaining hour, I daydreamed of living by the beach, taking acting classes, and working on a film set. I vowed to save money and move to California as soon as I graduated, to choose my dreams, to choose me over Bradley.

An unexpected chime directed my attention to the glass door. A stunningly handsome, six-foot-five man strolled inside. I had never seen this man in town or on campus, let alone in this store. I would have remembered him. Yet with the electric current coursing through my body, my inner being felt as if my soul recognized his from another lifetime.

Older than me, but maybe not quite thirty, his hazel-green gaze met mine and red heat raced to my cheeks. *Say something, oh yes, greet the customer.* That would've been a lot easier if my mouth hadn't suddenly filled with cotton as if I had just smoked Snoop Dogg out.

"Good afternoon," I said as I reached for a water bottle.

"Hi," he said, smiling as if he were just as transfixed.

When he turned away, I moved to sneak a quick peek of myself in the mirror and stubbed my toe on the trash can instead. *Shit.* I checked to see if anyone saw me, like I always did when something potentially embarrassing happened. I hoped he hadn't seen me lose control of my limbs. He packed so much heat, he needed to wear a warning label on his forehead. At least then I would've had something to stare at while I wrestled with the awkward teenager trapped inside me.

He screamed "bad boy," the type of guy who wasn't good news at all except for maybe in the sheets, the type of swagger that instantly attracted me then. With the intensity in which he kept looking at me, there seemed to be more to him than just his edginess. His eyes spoke of a rapt awareness and to him having a story.

As I focused on this man, an overwhelming desire consumed me beyond the instantaneous attraction. Sure, I wanted to relinquish my self-control over to him and have him pull my hair at the same time, but beyond that, I felt an inexplicable connection and unfamiliar intrigue. Nobody else existed. Butterflies pranced as he browsed through the section of men's dress shirts, pausing every so often to eye me. I hoped I looked okay and took a quick—this time successful—side glance in the mirror. I longed for his tattooed arms to whisk me into the back office.

A woman's voice launched me into the realization that we weren't alone. Hyper-focused on him, I didn't realize the two of them had walked through the door together.

"I have some clothes on hold," the woman said.

"Okay, what's the name?" I asked.

"Lori Martin," she said.

"I'll be right back." I feigned gracefulness on my way to retrieve the requested articles.

When I returned, the lady said, "I decided to bring my son with me today since he's about six years behind fashion sense."

I paused, fingers midair while entering numbers on a calculator. The comment seemed a little odd, but I brushed it off rather than inquire further, more relieved to learn he was her son. Curiosity diverted my attention to the phone number portion of her handwritten, carbon copied receipt. *Should I save the number to call later?*

I handed him the shopping bag. A tingle ran up my body at the touch of our fingers. At the door, he paused to turn back. He opened and then closed his mouth as if he wanted to say something. I collapsed onto the counter when he departed, holding my head in my hands. Intuition reassured me this wouldn't be the last time I saw Mr. Mystery, and somehow, I also knew that, once again, my life would never be the same.

A few days later, a phone call from Kassie, a coworker of mine at the boutique, interrupted a mid-afternoon study session. She muffled into the phone, "Yourmanishere."

My heart raced at the mere mention of Mr. Mystery.

"Kassie, if this is some cruel, belated April Fool's joke, I won't hesitate to shove a stiletto in your ass. Don't make me ruin my shoes!"

"After hearing about him for the past three days—mind you, even on our girl's night to see Alicia Keys—I promise. I'm serious," she said. "Woman, he came back to the store just to get your number. I'm calling you from the office to ask if it's alright to give it to him, but mainly to tease you a little bit."

"Why are you still on the phone, madwoman? Write down my number this very second."

I hung up and tried to go back to studying, unsuccessfully.

She called back giggling, and the door chime announced his exit from the store in the background. While thanking her, call waiting beeped and an unknown number flashed across the caller ID. *Damn, that was quick.* The call shattered any remaining trace of concentration for studying.

"Hey. It's Chris, Chris Martin," he said.

Man, what a deep voice, a raspy sexiness.

"I got your number from a girl at your work. She told me it'd be okay if I called?"

"Y—yeah! That's quite alright, Darlin'...How are you?"

Darlin'? Since when was I a little southern belle? Gah, überdork.

"Well, good. Any plans for the evening? I'd love to take you to dinner," he said.

Sitting on my bedroom floor, flanked by numerous psychology books and the impending certainty of the next day's exam, I said, "I'm actually pretty free. Where do you want to go?"

There went playing hard to get.

"You choose. Anywhere you want to go," Chris said, "But I have to be honest with you. You'll have to pick me up. I'm in the process of getting a car. I'd take my mom's, but I haven't had a chance to get my license either. I don't wanna risk getting pulled over and getting into trouble or going to jail on our first date."

What did he mean by getting into trouble? And he already thought there was going to be more than one date? Who was I kidding? Schwing, yes!

"I can pick you up. What time were you thinking?"

"Seven?"

"That works. I'll call you for directions when I head your way."

I waited to hear him hang up before lying back on my floor, stretched out like a starfish onto the cloud of romance—*ahhh.* The alarm clock on my nightstand displayed four hours until my hot date.

After changing outfits numerous times, I stood in front of a full-length mirror. Reaching into my shirt, I lifted my boobs to make sure each stood perked at the height of attention. I placed my hand on my stomach while inhaling to appear thinner. On an exhale, I grabbed my purse to leave. I paused when my hand touched the light switch. With the scattered clothes on the floor, it looked as if a category F3 tornado had swept through, but I decided against cleaning my room in hopes the mess reinforced my intention of not giving in to any naughty desires that may formulate after a few cocktails. At least the mess would give the impression that I hadn't expected an encounter to happen.

I turned up the music as soon as I climbed into my Mazda Tribute. With each dance and shake of my arms, I released the anxiety. At a red light, I texted Chris for the address. A couple walked hand in hand on the sidewalk, leading me to daydream about what kissing him would be like. Instead of responding to my message, he called.

"Hey, this texting thing is still pretty new to me," he said. "A phone call is much easier."

His frustration with texting was an eye-opener. My dad always emphasized how many wrecks he saw from his eighteen-wheeler; I didn't need to text and drive anyway. Maybe Dad would approve. His aversion to texts was old-fashioned, but also refreshing since calling was more personal and present.

He guided me to their house with help from his mother's directions. Jitters accompanied me inside the beautiful red brick countryside home. Entranced as soon as I saw Chris, I smiled and noticed he was wearing the black shirt from the boutique. The rolled sleeves exposed his tattoos, and the ink enticed me with stories I had yet to hear. He led me into the living room, and I relaxed when his mom, Lori, properly introduced herself.

"Would you mind if I take y'all's picture before you leave for dinner?" she asked, a silver digital camera dangling around her wrist. I had no objection, but I didn't think this ever happened on a date outside of high school.

She held the digital camera up to eye level, "Act as if you like one another, sheesh."

Oh, that won't be hard at all, Mama Lori.

"Mom," Chris said, "this is embarrassing."

"It's okay. I don't mind," I said.

He relaxed and put his arm around me. I melted into the spot next to him. She took several more photographs similar to the ones a couple would take on prom night. I glanced over my shoulder at him as we walked to my car, and it took all I had to conceal my excitement. When I turned on the main highway, Chris said, "So where'd you choose?"

"I'd love to go to Shoguns! Craving sushi, but they have hibachi too."

"...Sushi? Okay, that's where we will go," he said.

"Is that okay? They have other foods besides raw fish."

"Oh, I know. Yeah, it's just hard to believe I haven't eaten there in over six years."

"Six...years?" I asked with a little trepidation.

I looked over, hoping he'd elaborate with more than just the vertical shake of his head.

"Okay...Did you get food poisoning there or something?" I asked.

He sighed. "There are some things I want to tell you. I want to be honest with you and upfront from the jump, but I'd like to do it over dinner if you don't mind? I want you to know my story in its entirety so you feel 100 percent comfortable if things should move forward."

"I admit...I'm really curious, but that's okay," I said. "And thoughtful."

"Especially since some of my past looks worse than what it is. If you were to hear about it, and let's face it, you would in this small town, I want you to hear it from me firsthand."

The honesty was foreign and somewhat uncomfortable. Although impatient, I nodded my head to further reassure him. I thought about what I may not want him to know, like having a sugar daddy.

I smiled, swinging my purse to and fro, as we sauntered across the busy parking lot to the restaurant's entrance. For the first time in a while, my smile wasn't a cover-up for any darker emotions on the inside, the feelings I believed most people experienced to some degree, but somehow weren't socially acceptable to display in public. Were only women destined to be Stepford wives, acting and doing on behalf of others, contorting into someone else's ideal portrayal while hiding the shadow parts away for themselves? Their behavior didn't seem like it was for themselves. Where was the raw emotional connectivity? Why did we pretend we didn't have insecurities or that we had life all figured out? Was it not safe to display emotions? If we showcased them, did we risk being labeled reactive, selfish, or crazy? I recognize now I asked questions of others that I could've asked myself, and I see the irony in wanting to trap myself.

"Two please," I said to the inattentive hostess, who looked up at me as she hid her cell phone underneath a menu.

She smiled before saying, "Right this way."

She placed two menus at a long, square table where other diners would soon fill the surrounding empty seats. My eyes lingered on Chris's. I wondered if he read my mind when he placed his hand in mine. It took a moment to realize the waitress was standing beside us.

"Ma'am? Something to drink?" she asked. "Ma'am?"

"Oh. Please. Mai Tai," I said, already tasting the blended rum and juice.

"Iced tea for me," Chris said and grinned ear to ear.

"Long Island or Firefly Tea?" the waitress asked.

"Unsweet," he said.

Dammit, should I have not ordered alcohol? The waitress nodded, leaving us alone with my embarrassment. As if he read my mind, he said, "It's okay."

He took my hand and turned it over, face-up, as that tingling sensation ran up my arm and through my shoulder. "You know," he said, "I'm a pretty good palm reader. I've read a few books while—"

"Nope, no. You can't tell me what you did in the car and avoid the conversation now. Out with it," I said. "I'm on the edge of this wooden seat and not looking for a splinter."

He took a deep breath. "There's no other way to say it," he said.

Please don't tell me you have three kids, a wife, or a—

"I just got out of prison," he said as he stared straight into my eyes.

Everything clicked. All the tells slid into place. The fashion sense, the texting, the car situation, the restaurant remark.

Curiosity filled my mind with so many questions of a world I knew nothing of. I was a little disappointed upon learning the information of his recent release. I had a penchant for boys with a little edge, but, prison, *actual* prison...this was a first. Mom was going to be so proud. Ha, oh lord. I reasoned with myself, justifying his actions, as long as the crime wasn't anything too heinous. I liked to believe in the good in people. I mentally gave him kudos for the honesty.

"I can tell by the look on your face that you're a little surprised," he said.

Still interpreting my emotions around his revelation, how was I to word a response? Had he given me this information on the phone, I could have processed the news on my own. I could've meticulously calculated a decision of whether to flee or stay. How could I weigh all of the pros and cons when sitting across from this green-eyed fire of intrigue? I felt like running right into the flames. I knew why he'd waited; he knew I wouldn't say no.

"I don't really know what to say. You dropped a bomb on me. What did you...?"

"Go to prison for?" he continued. "I'll tell you everything."

"Well, I'm surprised," I said. "I've never dated anyone who has been to prison. But I'm glad you are honest with me. Seems like a rarity these days. And honestly, if you would've told me over the phone, I don't know if I would've gone out with you. There's just something that pulls me toward you. I normally wouldn't even say that out loud."

"I feel the same. That's why I wanted to wait to tell you in person."

"It's a good thing I didn't google you," I said.

Did he know what I meant by "google"? How many references would he not understand? I liked the idea of stepping into a teacher role. The waitress returned with our drinks.

I sipped a long swig of the Mai Tai as he conversed with an older, tattooed lady who'd joined our table with her girlfriend. As they inquired about each other's tattoos, I admired their lack of judgment toward one another. I had one tattoo hiding under the threads of my shirt, "karma" written in large cursive letters along my right rib cage. At the time I chose the tattoo a couple years earlier, I had heard the ribs were the most the painful area of the body to receive one on. And honestly, that's why I chose the location. I wanted to be the badass girl who chose pain. As the needle ran across my skin, I found a numb, Zen-like home in the pain. If I could endure the tattoo, I could endure anything. I didn't know true pain then, but I would soon enough. Pain would choose me too.

Chris's eyes drilled into mine, daring me to look away. I met his challenge for a few moments before looking down at his arms and noticing a distinct difference in the ink saturation when comparing his arms with the older lesbian's arms. His tattoos displayed intricate detail, but the ink was a lighter hue. Her ink was a deeper black.

"Did you have all of these tattoos before you went to..." I said, glancing around, and then in a lower voice, "...prison?"

"No," he said. "And you don't have to whisper."

"Tattoos are allowed in prison?"

"Not many people care about following the rules in prison," he said.

Touché. Chris and the older woman continued to share ink stories as the chef prepared chicken, shrimp, and fried rice in the center of our U-shaped table. My body temperature increased every time he mentioned his recent parole at the hibachi table, at least five or six instances. The layers of my comfort zone were being peeled away by this man. Glad I could blame the redness of my skin on the heat of the chef's flame, but did he have to tell everyone? Why did I always care what others thought?

Maybe by being with Chris, I'd learn how to not care so much about others' opinions, like he demonstrated. Maybe the freed prisoner could teach the one still imprisoned. Maybe he could set me free. It'd be years before I'd learn that I was the only one able to liberate myself.

He continued his calm tale of the methods used for administering a tattoo at a maximum-security unit. "You see," he said, "you take an ink pen and a battery..."

The waitress placed a roll of sushi on a rectangular plate in front of me. I ripped the black and white paper from my chopsticks and rubbed the bamboo pair briskly in my hands to ward off any bad luck before picking up a piece of the roll. I didn't know what good sushi was then, but the spicy mayo and eel sauce combo would still dance on my tongue in a *closed eyes and moan* type of way.

"Here, try this. So fresh and so good," I said, holding a piece of the roll in the air.

"Okay, okay...one bite," he said with that sly, sexy smile. "My stomach has a little difficulty with flavorful food. I got used to eating bland food."

A look of delight crossed his face when I fed him the sushi, and I loved feeding him pleasure.

"Wow. That's delicious. It's actually my first time eating sushi," he admitted.

I thought about the drastic differences in our lives. So many simple things I took for granted, like the ability to choose a restaurant and eat whenever I want. He told our table a story of surprising his mom in San Diego, where she'd moved after rehab, with her name tattooed across his lower neck. I was relieved the woman's name on the lower portion of his neck was indeed his mother's and not a former flame's. A girl could only make so many concessions.

Chris had been home all of two days before we'd met at the boutique. Released on parole with a year left to serve on a seven-year sentence for possession of a controlled substance, he adhered to the rules and abided by all of the restrictions, at least for the time being. Chris and Lori were the black sheep of a prominent family in Tyler. I'd later come to know and love all of Lori's story as she became something of a second mother.

Only a month had passed dating Chris before I began to abandon my wants and needs in favor of spending time with him. It was as if any affection from a male spurred me into a self-negating spiral. I'd peel myself out of Chris's bed in just enough time to make my classes. I started skipping workouts and told myself we'd be getting enough of one in the sheets. I quit my job at the boutique, cushioned with a small savings and the notion that I'd soon receive graduation gifts.

Entranced by the energy of Chris, my world became him. His world became mine. Love-drunk and not desiring sobriety any time soon, he and I were inseparable—eating, sleeping, showering. I lost touch with my need for personal space. I accompanied him on his parole visits and introduced him to all of my friends. No other future existed other than the one with Chris and me conquering life together.

The distance between Dallas and Tyler helped place space between the feelings for Bradley. With no idea of polyamory and zero concept of an open relationship on my radar, I battled with myself. Could I love two people at the same time? Was that even possible? Selfish? I measured my relationships next to what the other people around me were doing and lived in a constant state of comparison. I hated replicating my mom's and Bradley's actions of keeping two people on the line, yet there I was, torn between my love for Chris and Bradley. I wanted them both, and I wanted to exist in a world where I wouldn't hurt either. That world didn't exist, but for a time, I lingered with the one who hadn't hurt me yet.

Days before my graduation in May of 2010, in a dressing room at Saks Off 5th on Park Lane in Dallas, Chris and Colin waited for me to model a dress. My phone buzzed—a text from Bradley. Silencing the tone, I threw the BlackBerry into my purse.

"Just a sec," I said and rotated away from the mirror, unable to look myself in the eyes. I shimmied into the white and gold dress, struggling to zip up the back. I stepped from the room to stand in front of the three tall mirrors and turned in a circle. The dress accentuated my hips and breasts without being too revealing. I felt like a Greek goddess—on the outside, anyway, and that's what mattered at the time.

"Wow," said Chris. He wrapped his arms around my waist and kissed me. "Stunning."

"Definitely the winner," said Colin.

Chris glanced at the price tag on the one-shoulder Calvin Klein dress and asked, "How are you affording all of this, babe?"

Colin, the only person privy to my secret, glanced at me and stood, "I'm gonna go find the perfect shoes to match."

"Graduation money, babe," I said. *Liar, liar, liar.* Who knew that truth-telling was a great first step to a life of authenticity?

Back in the dressing room, I scrolled through the messages on my phone and read the last one. I worried Chris would leave me if I told him about Bradley or my past and felt pressure to decide to spend the rest of my life with Chris or hang around for a possibility with Bradley.

Bradley: *"wired $ to your acct today, proud of you angel love"*

"Thanks, hun," I replied, before deleting the message.

A few days later on graduation night, after I walked across the stage, I scanned the swarm of people. I'd invited Lonnie to the ceremony and waited for him to approach my group of supporters: Mom, Dad, Christopher, my new stepmom Ann, and my dad's mom, Nana. I wanted to hug Lonnie and look into his eyes, to feel the pride emanating from them, and to know he still loved me. Later that same evening, Lonnie texted to say he was in the crowd but felt too awkward to approach.

"Lonnie," I responded. *"Just because your relationship ended with my mom, doesn't mean ours has to. You've been a father to me for more than a decade. Let's get together soon."*

Afterwards at the celebratory dinner, I introduced Chris to my family after a month of dating. My family astonished me with how accepting they were of him, which probably upset me too since a part of me loved getting a rise out of others. After all, if their feelings rose, they were demonstrating they cared for me.

History really does have a funny way of repeating itself until a lesson is learned. Immediately after graduation, instead of moving to California to pursue my writing and acting dreams, I moved in with Chris and Lori. Banking on our whirlwind romance, long-term plans were lost to the thrill of the moment. What could go wrong?

I exhausted excuse after excuse for not visiting Bradley, and after a bit of hesitation and much inner deliberation, I communicated that I had met someone. Bradley responded, "*I respect your honesty, but I'll be here when the beau du jour's gone.*" Anger traced through my veins, every ounce of me hoping to prove him wrong.

Chris mirrored my rage, having quit his bipolar medication cold turkey. I shoved away any concern and chalked our heated arguments up to passion. His biting remarks stirred my emotions, acting as triggers for all of the anger that I hated to feel. Anger wasn't an emotion a good girl was *supposed* to feel, how women are often conditioned to behave. I shamed myself every time the rage rose, especially if the feeling incited a verbal diarrhea type of reaction. I didn't know then that allowing someone else to control your emotional state was a choice to give them your power, or that I could respond instead of react.

After graduation, the passion between Chris and me only grew in intensity. We made love to feel the heat. We argued to feel the heat. And then we argued some more. I'd taunt him with my eyes as he glared with a darkness in his own: *What are you going to do, hit me?* I masked everything as fine in a similar manner to how Lori hung framed pictures on the wall to conceal the holes he'd punched.

The heated back and forth disagreements discombobulated me. I hated confrontation and charted foreign waters within myself, shocked every time my flustered emotions compelled me to respond by yelling. I see this now as emulating the love my parents had modeled from one of my first memories. Chris's behavior triggered me but also offered the opportunity to heal a childhood trauma. The people around us offer a purview, a mirror into our own healing. If we dare peek to examine the triggers and similarities, we give them the opportunity to serve as teachers.

On many levels, Chris took me to places I'd never ventured. He stepped on every trigger button and later licked his way to forgiveness by going down on me for an hour. We cried after experiencing simultaneous orgasms, the first I'd ever experienced during sex. I labeled our disagreements as lovers' quarrels. Looking back, he wanted proof of my love and to fill an adolescent emptiness from when his mom was in rehab. Maybe I wanted the same from him. After reading countless self-help books, I understand now that I accepted the love I thought I deserved and attempted to repair childhood traumas by my subconscious selection and attraction to certain men.

On a summer evening in July, Chris bounded into our room. "Who bought your Lexus?"

The curve of the truth met the curve of my lips. "I told you I used money from my dad."

A dad of sorts.

"Why can't you just fucking be honest with me?" he yelled.

Because I'm not honest with myself.

My voice rose to match his, "I don't know what you're talki—"

He held up a journal and some loose papers. "I found these in your glove box."

I'd locked my closest thoughts away in a place I doubted he'd look. He tossed them at my feet, where I felt my stomach had landed.

"Why are you going through my things?"

"Because your stories don't make sense. You quit your job. You have an endless supply of cash. Are you cheating on me?"

"It's not like that, I swear," I pleaded.

"Then what the fuck is it like?" he asked.

"You sure as hell don't have a hard time helping me spend the money."

"You know I've been trying to find a job," he said.

"Oh, at the lake with me?" I yelled. "Or on our trip to the casino in Shreveport?"

Lori walked into the room and stood between us. "This. Has. Got. To. Stop. I will *not* continue to have the peace disturbed in my house. Either figure this out or we're going to have do something else."

She pointed her finger into Chris's chest and locked eyes with me before shuffling in her slippers down the hallway. A couple long, painful minutes of silence passed, stretching me closer to the truth.

"Will you sit with me outside?" I asked.

Staring at the pasture behind the house, I waited for him to sit beside me on the brown wicker patio loveseat. I rested my elbows on my knees and fought back waves of nausea. "I've been battling with wanting to tell you something. I was scared of losing you. Before I met you, I'd been dating this older, wealthy guy."

"A sugar daddy?" he asked.

"Y-yeah. He wanted me to travel with him...and wired money to be able to see him easier and have less stress. I worked at the boutique out of boredom. I swear I haven't slept with him since we've been together. I've texted him but haven't seen him. I feel like he's trying to lure me back, but I'm done. There. It's all in the open now."

I waited through what felt like an eternity of silence. "Will you please say something?"

"I've been honest with you from day one," he said.

"I know...I was afraid to lose you."

"You could've told me. I'd even have let you see him."

What? Did he just greenlight me seeing them both?

"Why don't we get out of town? Maybe visit friends in Austin?" I said, knowing a friend of his from prison had paroled there.

We decided to refresh our relationship after four months and packed for a road trip to the Texas hill country to visit friends and to float the San Marcos River. Patsy, a bubbly yoga instructor I'd worked with at a fitness center during college, had also recently moved to the area to attend Texas State University. With additional peace of mind from spending Bradley money on us, I reserved a room for us at the Omni for three nights in Austin.

Our first two days were fun and rather noneventful, making it seem like we could piece our relationship back together. But on our last day in Austin, we met up with Patsy for a river tube float. Patsy waved at us in her apartment complex parking lot, greeting us with a bright smile and platinum blonde hair. Once we'd pushed our inner tubes into the cool water, Chris tied a tube to float behind us and carry the blue Igloo cooler. Against his parole stipulations, Chris had started drinking a month prior, and unbeknownst to me, stopped taking his bipolar medication.

Patsy slowed her tube for a pit stop at "Shotgun Island," a cluster of rocks in the middle of the river known for being a good place to stand and chug a full beer. We laughed and stayed there for a couple of competition rounds. Texas country music drifted from passing floaters. We laughed and waved. Chris pulled on my foot and sucked my big toe, almost losing a tooth from a surprised kick of my foot.

Once Patsy was gone and we were on the way back to the hotel, Chris and I snipped at one another. Maybe it was the drinking, or the heat of the day and dehydration, but I blacked out during the drive. The next thing I remember, we were in our hotel room and at each other's throats.

"Show me your phone," Chris demanded.

"Why?" I yelled.

I couldn't remember if I had deleted all of my messages. Was there anything incriminating? With my cell phone in hand, I raised my hand in the air at the same moment he stepped closer to grab for the device. My hand met his face. He pushed me, and I shoved him back. I curled up into a ball on the bed with the phone still clutched in my hand. Chris flipped me over and tried to pry the device out of my fingertips while he sat on my waist. I wriggled and struggled against the weight of his body. He held me down on the king size bed by wrapping his hands around my throat. Cold, black eyes stared into mine.

Frightened by the sudden unfamiliarity in his eyes, I tried bucking and kicking him off. *He might accidentally kill me.* Just as my eyes lowered with heaviness, on the verge of passing out, a knock on the door saved me. Chris released his hands.

"Hotel Management," a voice said.

His body language morphed. He looked about the room as if searching for clues or pieces of the puzzle for what he'd done. I answered the door.

"Is everything okay in there? There's been a noise complaint. If y'all can't start getting along, I'm going to have to ask you to leave," the manager said.

"I understand, I'm sorry," I said. "We'll be quiet."

The manager mouthed, *Are you okay?* I nodded and closed the door. Chris and I stared at one another without uttering a word until he walked out the door.

Frozen, scared, embarrassed. Embarrassed that I'd become a woman with a tolerance for violence. I'd never had someone get physical. My mind raced, plotting my next move. *How would I get away from him? Where would I go? What would Chris do if I told him I was leaving?* I still had to sleep next to him and ride in a car with him back to Tyler the next day. I stood, pulled the red curtains back, and looked outside the window.

Chris walked beside the pool, illuminated by the moonlight and fluorescent lamp lights. In the elevator, I examined myself in its glassy mirrored surface. *How had I gotten myself in this position?* I pressed the down button to join him.

"I'm sorry," Chris said, choking through tears. He fell to his knees and wrapped his arms around my legs. "I'm so sorry."

"I know," I said. "I know."

I rubbed my hands through his black hair and stared at the empty pool and cabana. My heart ached, but deep down, I knew I was worthy of better treatment. I resolved to fake that we would recover, to do everything to get home and move out. But move where?

Chris drove us home the next morning, puzzling me with the way he laughed and sang and danced with such ease. The rate at which he had swept off the previous evening alarmed me. I didn't think I was *that* good an actress.

As we neared the house, I promised him I would tell nobody but aimed to remove myself from the situation before things could escalate. If something this horrific happened in a few months of dating, no telling what would happen later in the relationship. At this point in my life, in a less than rational state, moving to my mother's house and returning to the tiny town I'd escaped felt like a permanent failure. I also didn't want to sign a lease in Tyler and be tied to that rural town for another year. Distraught, I searched for a quick solution.

At the breakfast table the next morning, I chewed the bland scrambled eggs Chris had cooked. I sensed his eyes following my every move and placed my hand in his to convey my sincerity in staying.

"Thanks for cooking, babe. I'm gonna meet Kassie for CrossFit," I said, kissing his cheek.

Instead of going to the gym, I drove the Lexus in circles around Loop 323, and with each repetition, I felt like I was outlining a bull's eye target around my life. This was not what I had envisioned. *Everything would be better if I could just get out of town. I had to get out. I needed to run.* I didn't want Chris to know where I lived, and I didn't want to be in the same town as him. I pulled into the Target parking lot, called Bradley, and confessed what had happened, silently cursing that he'd been right about this relationship. This would be the first time, but certainly not the last, that Bradley came to my rescue. And in an odd similarity, he saved me like a father would save his little girl.

"Baby angel," he said, "Move up here...I've got an extra condo off Royal Lane. The remodel is almost complete."

Relief washed over my tense body, followed by an immediate hesitancy. *Does this obligate me to him whenever he wants?* Unkeen on the idea of him holding the condo over my head but with minimal savings and no job, my options seemed limited. I'd eventually learn to listen to my intuition more, at least without it having to knock me over the head with a frying pan, but I hadn't learned to trust the inner whispers then.

"Okay. Okay, I will. When can I come?"

As I walked through the door in the garage, I hadn't expected to see Chris sitting in the kitchen. I stopped in my tracks, my athletic shoe leaving a black mark on the tile floor.

"How was your workout?" he asked.

"Phew, gonna be sore tomorrow," I said. "Gonna hop in the shower."

The water shielded and rinsed away any doubts. I toweled off and walked into our bedroom across the hall, thinking of seeking refuge for a couple of days with my mom.

"I think I'm going to go visit my mom," I said.

His eyes flickered in panic. "Everything okay?"

"Everything's fine," I said, rubbing my hand along his arm.

A healing surrender came over me as I pulled into my mom's driveway and drove past the familiar pink crepe myrtle trees. In the overgrown pasture, the grass had faded to a dry yellow with no hints of its old brilliant green. Cows munched across the brittle field. A sliver of moon replaced the setting sun. A lone coyote yelped in the distance. Sitting on the white front porch swing, I swayed back and forth in the silence. Like a pendulum, I pushed backwards and wanted to forgive Chris, until I teetered forward and thought of moving away for a fresh start.

"Everything okay?" my mom asked as she sat beside me on the swing, rubbing her hand along my thigh and soothing my anxious nerves with her gentle touch. As I snuggled into the crest of her arm and shoulder, she wrapped her arm around my body to tell me that all would be well.

"You always come home to heal," she said as she kissed my forehead. "Remember, this too shall pass."

After three healing days with my mom, I arrived at Lori's home on a mission to leave. Although I'd later learn that forgiveness didn't mandate a person reenter my life, I understood forgiveness to be a relinquishment of self back then. At the time, I didn't realize I could forgive, cut ties, and cease communication. That'd be a lesson to learn in coming years.

Chris grabbed the laundry basket out of my hands and dropped the plastic bin on the ground. A couple of DVDs fell onto the concrete floor of the garage, cracking the cases of *Pretty Woman* and *My Girl*.

"Don't do this," he pleaded.

I walked inside and scooped a handful of my clothes from the closet, hangers dangling as I carried the bunch to my car. I fixed my eyes on the ground, afraid if I looked into his, he'd convince me to stay. A bewildered Lori tried to calm Chris.

"Ya sure y'all can't work this out?" Lori asked, pacing alongside as I walked to the car.

I shook my head and steadied on my mission, rationalizing that if I was going to be hurt, at least with Bradley, there'd be no physical evidence and I'd have a full bank account. Money equaled freedom, ignoring the invisible strings tied to those dollars, or the weight of the strings' expectations.

As I backed out of the garage, Chris collapsed to his knees, crying and punching the concrete floor. Lori dropped to console him and would later tell me she'd reassured him that he'd meet someone else, that my leaving wasn't the end of the world. She told me he said, "You don't understand. I don't want to live without her. I know she's not coming back. I just want to go back to prison."

And I've learned that often, when we put our whole heart into an intention, we become a self-fulfilling prophecy.

7

ater that same day, I waited in the parking lot outside the CubeSmart storage facility in Tyler to load my furniture with my dad and my brother Christopher. I wondered if it was hotter than the ninety-nine degrees my car displayed. Maybe there was no such thing as triple digit temperatures in Japan, where undoubtedly some brilliant engineer thought of everything but Texas heat. The familiar rumble of my dad's Dodge Cummins diesel truck broke my reverie. Hopping out to bear hug him, I lingered in his smell of Marlboro Reds, laundry soap, and diesel fuel.

"Ya pick the hottest day of the year to move?" my dad groaned but gave me a wink.

"Thank you for coming to help," I said.

My dad didn't prod with questions, as he was never a man of many words. Questions were what I craved, though, believing each sentence ending with that crooked exclamation point emoted curiosity and love. I still crave them to a certain degree, to have someone be inquisitive about the inner workings of my mind, to ask the inconvenient questions, and to want the honest truths. But ultimately, I loved that the man I cared for most showed up when I needed him, even if in the only way he knew how.

After the two-hour drive, they helped lift my furniture up a flight of stairs into Bradley's condo.

"Sure y'all don't wanna grab Tex-Mex? My treat," I said.

"Can't babe, got a load to Houston early in the morning. You be careful, kiddo. Drinking is a slippery slope."

"I'm careful, Daddy."

I hugged him goodbye, and not long after he pulled out of sight, I drove the few blocks to Bradley's home. A gorgeous arrangement of lilies and a "Christmas in July" Neiman Marcus clothes rack awaited. I sprawled across his white, leather couch and stared at the black, glass chandelier protruding from the white ceiling. Bradley slid a David Yurman ring onto my right ring finger, an onyx gemstone set with small white diamonds.

"I chose black to signify this stage and moment you're experiencing... but life will get better, angel love" he said.

"Thank you, I love it," I said, holding my hand up to examine the glittery promises that encircled the darkness.

Later, we embarked on a bowling adventure with a girlfriend of mine, Dylan. Several shots of tequila and gutter balls later, we were three giggling buffoons who had all managed to somehow win a round. Stumbling back to his house, drinks were made, and lines were laid. The tequila and beer did not sit right with my stomach, and even if I could have partied a little longer, I craved an early night. I hadn't given myself time to process all of the emotions, and I didn't have it in me to stay up and feign enthusiasm for any *unique* sexual requests. I played up my nausea and slept in an upstairs bedroom.

Dylan snored with her mouth open, waking me in the middle of the night. With an eye-squinting, light-piercing headache, I fumbled down the steps to the kitchen to retrieve my purse and hangover remedy concoction, but my purse no longer rested on the granite counter where I'd left it.

The clock on the upper oven read 5:00 a.m. A green pack of cigarettes rested on the fireplace, Newport menthols, a stark contrast to Bradley's blue and white Parliaments. Confused, I walked to his bedroom. When I reached for the doorknob to his room, a woman's voice greeted me through the door. *What the fuck?*

Hurt and outraged, I wanted to beat down the door, yell, kick, scream, throw a tantrum; but I froze, simultaneously petrified by confrontation and the knowing that, like maybe glimpsing your parents having sex, I wouldn't be able to unsee anything on the other side of the door. Instead, I moved the pack of cigarettes and laid them on top of his, an indirect gesture to alert him that I knew he'd invited another woman into his bed while I slept upstairs. *Was his plan for her to be gone by morning and I'd never know the difference?*

Around noon the next day, in an effort to console me, he tried to vindicate his actions with a nonfunctioning penis excuse. I'd experienced his erectile dysfunction firsthand, but in what realm did that justification meet the weight of having another girl in his home while I slept under the same roof? Being unable to sleep with her absolved his choices?

When the banks opened on the next business day, $5,000 appeared in my bank account. The money influenced my decision to stay tethered to Bradley, building resentment toward the both of us while pushing the truth down, way beneath the surface. I wasn't brave enough to be honest with myself yet. If his actions weren't low enough to be my breaking point, what would be? My self-worth and confidence would muddle lower and lower until I stopped recognizing who I'd become as a person. But, at twenty-two, a year into our relationship, I'd really only just begun the spiral downward.

The days and nights remaining in the summer of 2010 blurred together. My alcohol consumption distanced me from my writing and acting aspirations and allowed my dreams to be just a pretty little depiction I told myself the future held.

Even though my dad had cautioned me about alcohol by this point, drinking until blackout somehow falsely validated that I enjoyed life and lived it to the fullest. The buzz numbed my constant comparison to others. The feelings of not measuring up and not feeling good enough lubed my actions by lowering my inhibitions.

Bradley suggested that I rent the spare room of the condo to make a little extra money. With the constant flow of his wire transfers, I didn't fancy myself as needing extra money and hated being told what to do. So instead, Colin moved into the spare room without any expectation for him to pay. He helped decorate the condo—spending thousands on a couch, chaise lounge, artwork—and became my shopping companion, my dinner party guest, my drinking buddy, my driver.

I've since learned that the qualities we don't like in others may be something we dislike or ignore in ourselves. The exact expectation that I despised from Bradley was what I expected from a rent-free Colin— go and do what I wanted, when I wanted. Like myself, Colin would typically acquiesce and appease. We all pay it forward, but sometimes in ways we don't anticipate.

The only consistencies in my life were the wire transfers and my numbing behaviors. Bradley's money allowed a certain frivolousness in my spending habits. Colin and I day-drank and shopped, or night-drank and drugged. After drinks one evening on lower Greenville Avenue, I tossed Colin my keys to drive us home. At a yellow light, he turned the car down another street. White headlights approached us in the same lane. The driver honked their horn. He had turned down a one-way street, headed in the wrong direction.

"Colin, Colin!"

"Oh, fuck," he said.

I've learned life always reflects our inner essence, and the Universe will whisper before shouting. My life was metaphorically headed into oncoming traffic as well. He pulled into a parking lot while I checked the area for a cop car. "You good?" I asked him, a question better suited for myself.

When I plopped in my bed that evening, my fingers flew across the screen of my phone, fueled with Grey Goose courage. I squinted my eyes at the bright screen in my palm and typed, "*I miss you.*"

I woke the next afternoon. *Ex Idiot—Dont Answer*, what I had renamed Chris in my phone, appeared across the screen. And just like that, I started seeing Chris again, feeling safety within the walls of a home I could sort of call my own. He arrived, and after laying our "just friends" groundwork, I asked, "Where'd you go last night?"

"Gentleman's Club, where Sasha dances," he said.

I threw a piece of popcorn at him. "Look at this ring Bradley gave me," I said, holding up the onyx and diamond ring, hoping to provoke a response.

We tumbled and fooled around in my sheets, but because we didn't sleep with one another, my conscience stayed in the clear, à la Bradley's erectile dysfunction. The only dysfunction was the fact that I'd learned to barter with my body and call the process flirting. My body had become a tool.

Although an unintended consequence, Bradley's power over me influenced me to exert my own and manipulate people into doing what I wanted. Knowing what Chris craved, I withheld the goods from him regardless of my own desire. Scandalous, dangerous, unpredictable— I liked the power. My sexual interactions were something outside of myself. I didn't realize I'd become disconnected from my body.

Bradley called while Chris showered in my bathroom. He never called, so I answered.

"Hey baby, I'm driving by with a friend. Thought I'd swing by and introduce y'all."

"Sure, see you in a few," I said.

I dropped the phone on my bed, ran into my bathroom, and reached across Chris for the faucet knob to turn the water off.

"You've got to go," I said.

"Woah. What's up?"

"Now," I said and tossed him a towel. "Hurry. Bradley is on his way here."

Chris scrambled to dress and gather his belongings. I tossed him my keys.

"Hang out in my car. Ride around, whatever you want. Just go," I said.

He walked out the back door as Bradley parked in the front parking space. Adrenaline pulsated at my fingertips before circling back to my heart. I had barely caught my breath when Bradley knocked. I paused to collect myself before opening.

"Hi, baby," Bradley said.

As I closed the door, the contrast of his black Lamborghini Murciélago in a parking lot with no covered awnings rivaled my own feelings of being out of place. Both the car and I were pretending to be part of another world.

"This is Greg," Bradley said. "We're driving the new Lambo around and I wanted to introduce you."

As soon as they left, I texted Chris to let him know the coast was clear. He came through the door shaking his head in disbelief and asked, "Who parked your car last night?"

"Why?"

"It was angled a couple inches from the pole. The volume almost blew out my eardrums when I put the key in the ignition," he said.

"Oops," I said.

He picked me up in his arms. As I wrapped my legs around his body, we laughed about being a modern-day Bonnie and Clyde.

———

After another month of living in the condo, blacking out four or five nights a week, I could feel the disconnection and imbalance in my life. To course correct, I defaulted to what I was *supposed* to do, what I *should* do, what would please my parents, what seemed logical, and what could cushion my account with enough money and security to depart from the pull of Bradley's money. A job.

Hired as a full-time customer service representative, I started working at a high-end travel service company. The excitement of driving downtown and being a "big girl" barely lasted through the probationary month. At seventeen dollars an hour, I couldn't reason with selling a piece of my soul in a nine-to-five, patriarchal type of job. The irony being that staying attached to Bradley in our quasi-relationship felt akin to selling my soul too.

I know now it wasn't the exchange of time, energy, or companionship for money that squelched my soul. It was not respecting myself enough to leave despite the money. So logically, I sprinted to hedonism, a temporary appeasement that would take more and more to muffle the growing disconnection.

A few weeks passed, and while there were occasional movie marathon nights with Bradley, most of our time together laced drug-fueled evenings with dramatic experiences. Like one evening when I met him at Kirby's on Greenville Avenue for dinner and drinks.

Face bright and welcoming, he stood as I clicked my blue Christian Dior heels across the empty dining room floor, still getting accustomed to walking in four-inch stilettos. Rounds of vodka and whiskey led us back to his place. After I inhaled a rather large line from a glass mirror, his wide blue eyes held a little panic behind them. *What had I done this time?*

"Oh my. You just snorted Molly, pure MDMA," he said, pointing at the faint differences of two separate white powder piles.

Thirty minutes later, my eyeballs vibrated to and fro. The Rolling Stone portrait in his bedroom shifted left and right as if Mick Jagger himself were giving me a solo performance. My heart quickened for a couple beats and then slowed. Quick, quick, slow, as if two-stepping to techno. I doubted my heart's ability to steady and feared I'd lost myself to a version of *Fear and Loathing in Las Vegas*. Edging close to panic and on the brink of overdose, I craved normalcy and pleaded in one of those sudden Jesus moments where one prays and prays and promises to never touch the stuff again if you survive the evening.

Bradley guided me next to the glowing fireplace. "Come here, baby. Lie down. Everything is going to be okay," he said, his words a sweet lullaby. He traced his fingers along the small of my back and recited a Lord Byron poem.

"She walks in beauty, like the night
Of cloudless climes and starry skies;
And all that's best of dark and bright
Meet in her aspect and her eyes..."

Calming me seemed an effortless action for him. I believed his reassurance proved he truly cared about me because he pushed aside all of his sexual desires for the evening. Despite me circling Pluto on drugs, his tenderness and vulnerability satisfied a longing for the connection we'd shared in Mexico. That feeling was the home base I longed for. Those moments of hope kept me around and further established our back-and-forth pattern. I didn't know then, but a disconnection was growing between my mind and my body.

While I despised the objectification and the belittling of my intelligence, I ignored the rage that sprouted in me when he told me I was pretty when I asked a question or when he called my body parts toys, pacified by the adoration I interpreted as love. The sex, money, and desire stroked my ego. I heeded his every sexual wish, detached and disassociated from my choices, and sunk into silence. Objectification was a thing he did to me; I never checked myself for the same cancer. Yet my silence, self-judgment, and shame fed the emotional malignancy.

I contributed to my objectification by placing my value on my appearance: the new clothes, the jewelry, and the experiences I could provide for myself and for friends. I numbed myself and slipped into a cadent addiction to the glamour, glazing over my truest desires as my trust in myself dwindled. Perched on the nest of him, too fearful and too hopeful to flutter away, I clipped my wings with a belief in my inadequacy and fear of the unknown.

> *"Some things scratch the surface while others strike at your soul."*
>
> —*Gianna Perada*

8

SUMMER 2010

About a month later, toward the end of that summer in Dallas, Lonnie reached out through a text. *"I bought a couple kayaks. Want to go up to Broken Bow Lake next weekend?"*

I'd always loved Broken Bow, Oklahoma. The town lies nestled between the Ouachita Mountains and the Red River Basin. Growing up, I imagined the Native Americans roaming the land and envisioned my ancestors of the Choctaw tribe hunting buffalo. Relating more to the captured prey than the empowered hunter, a part of me yearned for release.

My mom and dad had married in the area at Beavers Bend State Park. One of my favorite photographs, and maybe one of my most prized possessions, was them gazing at one another with their hands placed on a delicate, white bible on their wedding day. I liked to think I'd been conceived near those waters. But maybe that is me now seeking to find the poetry in one of my life's hardest moments, hoping a dark beauty rests in the lands where a piece of me would also die.

I interpreted Lonnie's message as him still caring about me despite how my mom ended their marriage. He must have shared my feelings and respect for the history we shared for him to want to maintain our stepfather–daughter relationship.

Lonnie had been sober for almost as long as I'd been alive. Twenty-plus years. And I'd been craving a break from drinking, but I didn't even know then that I had a problem with saying no. Not just with booze, but with everything and everyone. An underlying sense of obligation that I owed something to everyone hindered my growth. I sensed other people's expectations and worked hard to meet or exceed those expectations, to validate my existence with a fleeting feeling of love or acceptance. And like with an out-of-reach itch, I twisted and maneuvered to get closer and feed the urge to scratch. I hoped to catch up with Lonnie, have one of our old philosophy or quantum physics talks, and maybe ask him questions about his sobriety.

Bodies of water calm my being. The idea of escaping the highway, sirens, and other city sounds of Dallas sounded divine. I could already see the lightning bugs in the night air, hear the singing cicadas, and smell the *OFF* mosquito repellent spray. Plus, I'd have a legitimate excuse for weekend plans if Bradley asked to see me.

After driving to Lonnie's house in Pittsburg, Texas, I hopped in with him for the remainder of the two-hour road trip to Oklahoma. On our way to Broken Bow, the sun glistened in through the front cabin of his blue Ford Explorer Sport Trac, illuminating a faint crack in the dash leading to the radio. I reached to twist the volume knob to the right as I sang along to a Foreigner song.

Lonnie drove along the winding S curves, tracing the guard rails and pine trees as we neared the Texas and Oklahoma state line. There was a lightness; everything looked green despite summer coming to a close. Driving the main drag of Broken Bow, we passed the Indian slot machine casino and the Piggly Wiggly grocery store. Growing up, the Piggly Wiggly was our annual camping trip's fill station where I'd sneak candy into the wobbly cart my dad pushed. We turned right into Beaver's Bend and passed the familiar gravel road leading up the mountain to my family's favorite old campsite, the same spot where my mother and father honeymooned after their shotgun wedding.

The scenery sprouted old memories. As a family, we'd stop in the nature center where the caged, wounded owls entranced and fascinated me. How I longed to liberate the nocturnal creatures.

I smiled, recalling my freshman year of high school, when my dad, brother, and I strung a line between trees for wet clothes to dry after an unexpected downpour paused our tent assembly. We'd taken shelter in his Dodge. My brother and I had laughed as he cursed and combed his black hair back in the rearview. How confused I was when, on that same trip, my dad carried a bar of soap to the water, not comprehending how he'd get clean from the lake water. Maybe that's because I'd once pooped in the same lake when I was six. Sophisticated even back then.

Each camping trip with my dad was held during the sacred months of summer. Throughout the years, we bonded over our shared love of water. Kayaking the river in junior high, water skiing, or tubing behind my dad's boat in high school while I yelled, "Don't slingshot meeeeeeee," but loving when he did. Tumping his kayak when going down the three-foot waterfall drop, or the time he yelled at me to walk down to the bank of the riverbed. "Get down from there," he'd yelled as I climbed the tall tree swing.

"I'm eighteen, Dad, I can do whatever I want," I said, pushing away from the pine tree.

How the icy chill of the water met my skin and stole my breath. How I hated for a split second that he might've been right.

My recollections paused when Lonnie pulled up to the log cabin he had rented—a small, one-bedroom studio in the woods. Thinking nothing of the single bed, I unloaded groceries onto the kitchen table, and put away the dry coffee creamer in the open cabinets.

"This was all they had available," he said.

"It's cute. Quaint. I love it," I said, opening and closing doors, scoping out the bathroom, flicking lights on and off before asking, "Should we head to the lake now?"

"Burning daylight. Ready if you are," he said, clapping his hands together.

"Gonna grab my hat and sunscreen. Meet ya at the truck," I said.

On this beautiful, hot day in August, the water lapped gently at the shoreline with not a single cloud in the blue sky. I tightened my baseball cap before easing the kayak into the water near a blank cove. The brown mud covered my toes in grit and fine mussel shells. I waded further and dipped below the water to cool off before hopping into the kayak and paddling away from the shady cove. Oily water droplets formed on my arms as I lathered and reapplied the sunscreen to my wet skin. Scanning the scenery, the pine trees surrounded the water and enclosed the man-made lake in a tree cocoon. All was well.

Several hours later, after returning to the cabin to rinse the lake water off, my hair wet, I sat next to Lonnie in a rocking chair on the cabin's porch. He smoked a cigarette as the sun collapsed behind the trees, illuminating the sky with wondrous oranges and reds. I was soothed by his silent, calm presence.

After dinner, I watched a crime show on the older television set across from the queen-sized bed. Exhausted, I fell asleep long before my hair had a chance to dry.

I woke in the middle of the night. A presence hovered above me. Every cell and muscle in my body froze. I held my breath, unable to fully exhale until almost ten years later. *Did we forget to lock the door? Did the crime show seep into my subconscious sleep?* I kept my eyes closed, unsure if I should alert the person that I'd woken. I hoped Lonnie had packed a gun for the trip. Fingertips traced the space between my breasts then crossed over the delicate area above my heart. *Please let this be a dream. Please.*

The finger lifted, waited. Keeping my eyes closed, I rolled over like a casual toss or turn of a deep slumber, turned my back to the intruder, and curled into the fetal position. I felt like the scared little girl whose mind used to make witch's fingers from moonlit tree branch shadows in her window. I pleaded for the witch's fingers to take me with her into the darkness, to save me, rescue me from this reality. My breath hollowed and the shadows expanded, crawling across the comforter to bring honey for my fear. I laid there a scalped child, buried to the neck and awaiting the ants who'd leave nothing but the bare-boned truth. I braced myself for darkness but was only met with the terror of reality in the room.

The cabin's wooden door opened and closed. The light slam and creak of the screen door followed. Peeking above the pillow, I searched for Lonnie's form in the bed. It was empty. *No.* From the window, the red ash from the lit end of a cigarette burned while he paced the creaky, wooden porch. Footsteps approached the door. *No.* I rolled over to face my back toward the blank spot before he walked back in the cabin. I opened and closed my eyes a few times to ensure I wasn't dreaming. *No.* I craved the peace that sleep brings and prayed I'd be able to relinquish myself to the darkness. All the beauty of a place—and a person—I loved was suddenly tainted.

The next morning, skinned and raw, I dreaded the drive back to his house to retrieve my car. Maybe if I didn't acknowledge the previous night, the hurt and the pain would wilt. After we loaded our belongings into his truck, he stopped at a catfish restaurant for lunch. *How fitting, lunch with bottom feeders.* I forced an attempt at conversation, pushing the pinto beans and coleslaw around on my plate over and over with an old fork. My appetite just as lost as my belief in the person sitting across me. I don't know why I attempted small talk at all. How could he act so normal? But then again, how could I? Every time I acted in a way that negated my boundaries or silenced my words, I tore down a piece of the bridge that paved the way back to myself.

Betrayal burned the fringes of my soul until I sat sweating in the passenger seat. I fixed the air conditioning vents to face me directly and wiped the palms of my hands onto my pants, barely tearing my eyes from the road on the torturous two-hour ride to Texas, grimacing every time Lonnie inched into my peripheral line of sight. I counted down the miles while thoughts crisscrossed and infiltrated any remaining peace.

Did every man see me as a beautiful object to be used however they pleased? If a man I'd felt completely safe around—able to turn to with any woe or question—did, why wouldn't the rest of the sex? Did anyone truly have pure intentions? How long had he seen me this way? The slumber parties, or the times I ran around the house in my sports bra. How I sucked in the lower portion of my belly while examining myself in the mirror and how he'd told me I'd be beautiful even if I wore a potato sack. How when I pleaded for an answer to why nobody in high school asked me on dates, he said, "If you could only walk a few steps behind you, Little Deer, you'd see how they are intimidated." Did he have any of these desires then? Why. Why. *Why*...had he done this to me?

Did I wear something provocative? Did I suggest or hint in the slightest that I was interested in him?

Rocks crunched beneath the tires, indicating that his truck had pulled into his driveway. With my hand waiting on the door handle, I jumped from the truck before he came to a full stop, leaving only the sweat stain on the seat to indicate where my body once was, like a white chalk outline etched onto pavement. I tossed my overnight bag into my car and painted a smile on my face as I fought tears.

"Don't wanna come inside for a little bit?" he asked.

"No," I said. *You know what you did. I'll handle the hurt on my own.*

Facing one another in silence, his eyes pleaded with mine before reaching the ground, as if begging me to lock the terror in a vault. And I would hide the wound within my heart for years, but at that moment, I knew that he knew I knew, and that was all I could handle. I got in my car and backed out of the driveway in what would be the last time I'd ever see Lonnie.

I cried on the way back to Dallas, feeling like I'd lost a father. But unlike a death, there was no comforting hug from another mourner. I didn't know who to tell, for I knew the hearts the news would break.

I resolved to hold everything in and buried the trauma, thinking I'd save my mom from pain if I kept the secret to myself.

While eating dinner alone that evening, in a desperate search to know why men saw my physical attributes as a meal for them to devour, I silenced the television and wished the images blaring across my mind would stop with the click of a button. The remaining foundation of a life I once knew crumbled and caved while I sat on my living room floor, back against the couch, and decided that'd be all men got of me—a shell. I pushed the white coffee table away with my bare feet. *Fuck this. If my exterior or body is all men see in me, then I'm going to use me to my advantage.*

With this intention, I'd hold the power and play their game better than they ever could. In that moment, frosting my emotions with a veil of iciness meant choosing to listen to my head, muting my heart, and playing on the power of my pussy. I knew my life would never be the same, but I didn't think it'd be greater.

Like the television, the wound would bounce and bellow, emitting muted cries underneath the image layer. I'd eventually yearn to be loved for the real me, for who I am on the inside. But, at twenty-two, I stepped into the role of being a conscious parasite in relationships, to use men for my desires since they seemed to use me in whatever way to fulfill theirs.

I neglected to process the pain and built interior cinderblocks of shame and torment, only to shallow my breathing on the descent to a dark place at the bottom of a once-loved lake. Forgiveness wouldn't be found until I realized my place wasn't to be a trophy buck mounted on a wall for admiration. Until I realized how desperately I needed freedom and autonomy. Until I found love for myself.

Adversity doesn't equate to failure, but years would pass before believing I experienced a birth that evening. For despite the betrayal, a resilience sprung to life. Lonnie had always encouraged me to write and use my way with words. For the longest time, I think a part of me didn't want to prove him right. Yet here I am and here I stand, able to see the beauty in the pain and hold gratitude for the man whose abuse initiated my biggest inner turmoil and transformation.

> "The scatterbrain,
> is a little like,
> the patter of rain.
> Neither here,
> nor there,
> but everywhere."
>
> —Lang Leav

9

Given how tuned in and how connected to my core I feel on most days now, my past choices seem like they were made by an entirely different person. After the evening in the cabin with Lonnie, I exonerated myself by ruthlessly justifying my choices until the actions felt as if they were someone else's. Everything in life happened *to* me and not *for* me, which couldn't be further from the truth, and is the polar opposite of what I believe a decade later.

I drowned myself in designers, desires, or drinks. With this incessant thought pattern, a victim mentality rooted in my subconscious, which would cause more harm than the initial trauma and was amplified by my own self-judgment and shame. I've come to understand the power of the mind, that thoughts become beliefs that become actions and then results.

Maya Angelou said, "When you know better, you do better."

I offer myself compassion and strive to remember that I did the best I could at the time. However, my intuition screamed at moments along my journey, gesturing toward a part of me that knew better, a feminine trait I hadn't learned to trust. I've learned that when I know better *and listen* to myself, that's when I do better. But at this point in my life, I listened to everyone but myself and continued diving into external solutions.

On the last Saturday night in August of 2010, with Bradley visiting Denver for the weekend, I two-stepped underneath the rhinestone saddle chandelier at Cowboys Red River, a huge honkytonk in Dallas. A man in a cowboy hat, wearing starched denim with a center crease and black ostrich cowboy boots, spun and twirled me across the dance floor.

On a break from dancing, I patted the sweat on my forehead with a black cocktail napkin and checked my phone. *"Flying home early. Come over? I want to see you,"* Bradley texted.

"Out with friends. If I make it home early, I'll come over. I'll let you know," I said.

With my newfound iciness giving me power, I enjoyed living in the yo-yo, believing an ambivalent response to be better than a firm no and leaving him longing and holding the desire even though I had zero intentions of visiting. If he were to express his anger in a typical temper tantrum, a deposit would soon follow.

Around two in the morning, after I'd washed my makeup off, I sent a text: *"Night babe, I'm crashing, call me tomorrow."*

"I hope you die soon," Bradley's message said.

"Selfish cunt," said another.

"You have till Jan to get the hell out of the condo," he said.

I assumed he was obliterated and didn't respond, but the messages hurt. I called a friend, who came over with tissues in tow. Counting backwards from one hundred like the sheep I pretended to be, I tried to sleep. *Did he really want me to die?* While resentment had built in me, I still believed I loved him. I just hated myself for it and numbed myself into ambivalence. Did he not care about me at all? Why was he being cruel? I was done...again.

When the banks opened on Monday, I received a $5,000 wire transfer.

The following month, I traveled to Los Angeles to scout the city, visit friends, and entertain my idea of moving. Ever since I'd visited California with my mom for my sixteenth birthday, it became the place where all my storytelling dreams lived.

I understand now that to alter your life course, a flat tire from the Universe is sometimes needed. Even though the trip was my pilgrimage, over a plate of cocaine the night before departing, Bradley volunteered to accompany me.

Drunk one evening at the Sofitel hotel bar, after I had red-lit a three-some, Bradley yelled for my "country bumpkin slut ass" to vacate his condo again, escalating the argument to the point where a kind stranger from Seattle offered to buy me a plane ticket home.

My inner defiance roared, but instead of acquiescing to his desire or my own victimized heartache, I resolved to not have bitterness ruin the remaining time in my dream city. So, I accepted when Tony, a friend who lived in Calabasas, suggested a beach adventure.

Bradley had called the hotel to suspend any additional charges to the room. Out of a fear of embarrassment for what he may have communicated to the hotel staff, I'd opted for a back exit instead of walking through the main lobby. So, when Tony's green Chevy Trailblazer pulled into my line of sight from the long line of valet cars, my body relaxed.

California's finest green or the Bob Marley–inspired music, or a perfect combination of the two, lifted my spirits and helped shake the anger and betrayal of the previous two days. The words from the Rebelution song "Courage to Grow" landed as if they had been written for me.

Tony rolled the windows down, and I glided my hand through the air as the wind whipped my hair around my face.

Exiting from the 101, Tony maneuvered his SUV along Malibu Canyon. Trusting the road that lay ahead of the thick fog, we wound through the hills and valleys to arrive at a vacant restaurant next to a deserted Zuma Beach. After a Ketel One vodka shot served as our version of a breakfast smoothie, we plopped on the sand with a nice buzz. With a side glance and a sly smile, Tony declared, "I'm goin' in."

Did he leave his mind back at the bar with the bill? The Pacific was cold all year round—but in October? But then I asked myself, would I remember the day I jumped in the freezing ocean or the day I sat out on the side? The Ketel One in me—and my spontaneity-loving inner kiddo—said, "If you go, I go."

He stripped to his boxers and darted into the blue water. I trailed after him in my blue thong skivvies and black bra, liberating myself from incessant and anxious thoughts. Jumping into the cold ocean grounded me within my body. The chill of the water welcomed me with an aliveness, a sweet release from mapping out or perfecting my actions. The momentum of the ocean water splashed into my face, buckled my knees, and pulled me to the bottom. For a moment, I succumbed to the rocky waves. But I stood, gasping for air and spitting out saltwater. Met with Tony's encouragement, I ran further into the ocean.

"Go under, go under," he exclaimed as the next wave approached.

As I dove beneath the surface, the waved rumbled past me and onto the shore. I surfaced, surprised I hadn't been pushed to the ocean floor. To get through the turbulence, I had to flow with the water, not resist the force.

Lying on our backs on the shore, adrenaline coursed through our veins. After dusting sand from the crevice of my inner thighs, Tony and I climbed up one of the large, jutting rocks on the beach. He pushed me against the rock wall and kissed me. With the saltiness of his kiss, I'd tasted a desire in someone, wanting nothing other than their company, momentarily relinquished from the quid pro quo of relationships I'd accustomed and conditioned myself into.

Tony and California, or the feeling I associated with them, resonated with me and helped me to see a different future—a possibility, a new route. I'd swum in the freedom of nonattachment and believed living in Dallas prohibited me from becoming the fullest expression of myself. Next to the water, my mind, body, and soul synchronized into what I'd later come to know as *being present*. Instead of judging or observing my life, I had participated in the flow. Distance seemed to be the answer yet again. I'd distance myself from life in Dallas attached to Bradley and be a better person. Life would be better in California, *more alive*. I'd be better in California and listen to my longings.

Less than a week after returning to Texas, Bradley wired $10,000 to my account and declared his wish to prove his adoration, reoffering the condo for as long as I wanted.

But I wanted out, and I wanted out yesterday. I hid my intention to relocate and transferred the money into a savings account. Part of me wanted to leave his keys with the security guard, change my number, and never look back, but the nice girl felt obligated to tell him...eventually.

I poured myself into moving to the "land of fruits and nuts," as my dad called California. Confidence built with every accomplished step of the plan. Unsure of which area to live in and outraged by the cost of living near the ocean, I secured a tiny studio apartment in Studio City and leased the space sight unseen. Within two weeks, I shipped my furniture, mapped a road trip with stops in Albuquerque and Las Vegas, and asked my friend Kristen to join me on the road.

Crossing the border into California, tears of relief spat out in sobs, as if my soul were doing the heaving, praising me for listening and shifting a little closer to myself. The move signified a realignment with my own desires. For the first time in years, I'd leaped with faith and chosen me, trusting in the strength of my willpower to stay away from Bradley. Choosing me, and strengthening the relationship with myself, would be a life lesson that would take years to truly set in.

*"I don't know where I'm going from here,
but I promise it won't be boring."*

—David Bowie

10

Journal Entry: November 2010.

It's funny how life tends to throw you little tests of strength when you least expect it, like have you learned this lesson yet? I look around my tiny studio apartment that still has a box or two yet to be unpacked and organized, but I can't help but feel relief. I may have divided my living space and quadrupled my rent, but it is mine and nobody can take this away from me. I have chosen a life with more simplicity and absolutely love it. I almost feel as if I have found myself, not so lost and consumed by the frivolous. I am so happy. Life here just feels right. I still have a love for the finer things in life, but the methods required alteration. Independence is key.

Bradley sent me a text, asking me if I miss him a little bit, even a teensy tiny bit? Of course I do, but I cannot allow myself to go around him again. Writing this helps to give me the strength to not go back. I just find it rather ironic that as soon as I call California my new home, he informs me that he will be moving here as well. I know Los Angeles is a big city but knowing that he would be halfway across the United States boosted my resolve. Space would have made it that much easier to stay away, but I've realized not everything is supposed to be easy.

Midnight whisperings and the lingering unanswered questions swirled inside of me. Shortly after moving into my studio apartment in the fall of 2010, an inner frenzy compelled me to log onto Facebook. Sitting on my brown chaise lounge, laptop perched on my lap and wine glass in hand, I clicked on Bradley's profile. A mutual friend had told me he'd reconnected with a former girlfriend—the woman on the wall of his house. I see now how I wanted to move on, but I also wanted him to miss me and to realize he needed me, that I wanted to be his spoonful of medicine, that I didn't fully believe in my ability to leave and thrive on my own.

My finger pounded the arrow squares of the MacBook keyboard. I moved my eyes closer to the screen.

Her and her bohemian clothes.

How skinny she was.

How radiant.

The smile on his face.

The giant ring on her left hand.

On that finger.

My stomach churned the jealous knots into bitter hatred. She appeared to be everything I wasn't and exuded what I craved. She looked so sure of herself. I clicked through all of their photos, finding a sick, satisfying pleasure in this social media torture. The details stuck out from each photo as I compared myself to the brunette beside a beaming Bradley, the version of him I'd only seen in rare glimpses.

Bradley had moved into a Hollywood Hills mansion, the house from the movie *Pulp Fiction*. I hadn't been in contact with him, but when he extended an invite for lunch at his new place, any and all resolve shot out of my body. He greeted me with one of those ass-out type of hugs and pecked my cheek as if he were kissing a long-lost aunt. He flicked on lights and muted the television to give a tour.

"You can see the ocean on a clear day," he said.

"Cool," I said, peering around the modern living room for a sign of the hiding elephant.

I wanted to bury myself underneath the cozy fur blanket strewn across the sectional couch, to escape this tortuous reality and use the blanket like a time portal back to my apartment. I regretted my decision to visit after the sight of me didn't spur him into the *right* decision of begging for forgiveness and choosing me. Why did I subject myself to this familiar pain? Although excruciating, the feeling of abandonment was at least familiar to my ego.

"Look, it isn't like you're crazy in love with me or anything, right?" Bradley asked.

The only gesture or sound I mustered was the slight shake of my head while I fought to not cry. I forced a smile and congratulations, but my lip quivered.

"I'm happy for you," I said.

"I think you'd really like her," he said. "You two would actually get along."

My glassy eyes set on the fireplace in the corner and the fact that I wasn't good enough.

"You know I'll always be here," he said. "If you ever need anything, ask."

Bradley confirmed what my online snooping had discovered: he was indeed engaged. I walked outside, dwarfed by the sprawling city of Los Angeles. Pangs of tormented loneliness and rejection validated my feeling of inadequacy. With Bradley ready to settle down, and even though I had left Dallas and him, I'd still wanted him to choose me.

A month or two later, in January of 2011, I toyed with the idea of moving home. In an effort to stay strong, I closed out the browser window on my computer for Dallas apartment listings. I read older blog posts and journal entries detailing the excitement for my move, aiming to draw on my eager anticipation for the future from when I wrote them. I visited the overwhelming feeling of joy from crossing the California state line. I searched for signs of hope through small gestures like having a stranger return my smile as I filled out job applications.

I smiled at everyone. My smile was an invitation, my way of saying let's be friends. But I had yet to meet anyone new and the walls of my Studio City apartment were closing in. Since the childhood move to Mt. Vernon, I'd grown accustomed to making friends easily. The lack of receptiveness surprised me. People seemed put off by a smile, as if I were deranged or had escaped a mental institution.

One weekend that same month, I visited a friend who had moved to Orange County. While sitting around his pool, he offered me pills while we smoked weed: "Want a Roxy?"

"What's that?" I asked.

"Oxycodone," he said.

Although I didn't know the strength of the dose, I popped one pain pill and pocketed the other. The effects kept ramping, even on the drive back to Studio City. Keeping it between the mayonnaise and the mustard, I focused on the yellow and white lines of the side streets to my apartment. My head floated on my neck like a bobblehead doll. Needing someone to keep me awake, I called Chris, and even though we hadn't kept in touch, he answered. I sensed a strain, a tone of irritation in his voice after he answered my call on the second ring.

"Hahaha. I'm floating. Woooah."

"What did you take?" he said.

"Why so serious? An oxycodone..." I said.

"Kristin!"

"...or two..."

"What the fuck. You shouldn't be driving. I'm talking to you until you get home."

"Please come visit me...I miss you. I'll pay for your flight. Or meet in Vegas?"

"I can't...I met...Listen, pay attention to the road," he said.

A neighbor walked behind her miniature Yorkshire Terrier with a bedazzled pink leash. I squinted, as if that would focus my depth perception as I pulled into the parking garage of my building. I don't remember going inside my apartment, and when I woke, my front door was unlocked. I must've walked straight to my bed and passed out without pausing to lock the front door.

I'd double-checked my locks to make sure they were bolted since I was a kid. The unlocked door frightened me. A wave of nausea surged. I ran to the bathroom and hovered over the toilet. Loneliness hung over my head like a cloud, raining a torrential downpour of pity. Leaning against the tub, I rested my head on the ledge and comforted myself with Chris's reaction, his concern for my well-being. Maybe he hadn't forgotten about me. A few hours later, he called to check on me.

"I'm sitting under a pound of bricks. The only thing that will make me feel better is if I take another pill. Nothing sounds good to eat. This is awful," I said.

"That's heroin. Eat some cookies and milk."

"Heroin?"

"Synthetic, but same thing. Take care of yourself, Kristin. And don't take another one."

I didn't. I'd finally found an edge I didn't want to cross.

Over the next month, with a new resolve to remain in California, I looked for a job and enrolled in acting classes. I walked into Yardhouse, a restaurant in Glendale, to apply for a waitress job. Accustomed to landing every job I'd ever applied for, the manager's hesitancy threw me off.

"What's your favorite type of beer?" the manager asked.

"...Shiner bock?" I squeaked.

The manager stared without saying a word.

"To be honest, I don't know much about beer, but I'd love to learn," I said.

"We'll reach out," he said.

Humiliation crawled over me like ivy climbing up a wall. I left knowing I wouldn't receive a callback for the job. Looking back, unaccustomed to the varying forms of rejection, I took everything personally.

By this point, my savings account had a nice cushion, but I feared losing the money. Even if I continued living on Raisin Bran Crunch cereal, the $1,200 rent, insurance, student loans, and bills would deplete the nest egg within four or five months. Every time I checked my bank balance, I feared its depletion. Once or twice a week, I treated myself to lunch or a movie, but I spent the majority of my time hibernating in my apartment.

Although I hadn't seen him since he'd suggested I meet his fiancée, Bradley wired money into my account on random occasions, which I interpreted as a *don't forget about me*. He offered support if I requested assistance, but I hated asking. Since he didn't need me, I didn't want to need him.

I sought distractions, and with a figurative wave of a loneliness wand, created a profile on Seeking Arrangement, a newer sugar daddy website that seemed straight to the point about mutually beneficial relationships. *You want to spend time with me, and I want you to spend money on me.* No room for any messy feelings. I had a dream to bring to fruition and bills to pay, and a horizontal life would bring in a hell of a lot more than waiting tables. Two birds, one stone.

After a few conversations with a man online, we met at his beachside condo in Malibu for dinner. Walking next to him barefoot along the water's edge, I dug my toes deep into the wet sand and savored the purples and blues of the fading sun. Each ocean wave brought a temporary bliss, a healing pause to the incessant, streaming thoughts. I lived in my head, in a place above but ever critiquing my body and actions. The bliss of the tide was a momentary understanding or separation from identifying with my thoughts. Amidst the approaching darkness of that evening, the fading the sun reassured me that I could make it, that I could make my dreams come true. Even if I'd only scribbled in my journal or stared at the blinking cursor of a blank page, I'd rise like the sun to greet another day. Day by day.

When the sun dipped below the ocean horizon, I followed the man up the steps to his condo. He cooked a healthy dinner that we ate on the floor, like a little carpet picnic with red wine. He pushed a strand of my hair behind my ear and kissed me. I yawned. He laughed.

The wine and waves seduced me into a nap. An hour or two must have passed when I awoke, groggy, a tone alerting me to a voicemail from my dad. I ignored the message. I didn't believe he'd deem my actions as the most honorable, and I'd never been able to hide the quiver in my voice when I lied.

The next morning along the shore, two seagulls flew across the water in the distance. One dove into the water for a fish, leaving the other bird behind. While strolling, my dad texted a request to call him when I had the chance. *Why was he being so persistent? Simply checking up on his little girl?*

A call and a text registered a little odd. He'd usually wait until I called him back. His impatience stirred an urgent desire to talk to him. For some reason, my stomach felt uneasy and seemed to point at other hidden areas. When he answered, his slow rasp collided with the crash of the ocean and the mounting nerves.

"Think the Cowboys will ever make it to the Super Bowl?" I asked.

"More like cowgirls, these days," he said.

A lull lingered from the chuckle of his own joke, between the sounds of his drawl. His tone carried a hesitation, as if pregnant with a secret. We made small talk, but I felt as if I were bracing myself for the birth of his secret.

"I, uh, went to the doctor, and they found a couple of tumors in my liver."

Tumors? The word echoed. Tumors, tumors, tumors.

"Tumors? What's that mean? Ca-cancer?" I asked.

"Well, if it looks like a duck, walks like a duck, and quacks like a duck, it's probably a duck."

Cancer? How could this happen to my strong, fifty-seven-year-old dad?

Life became monotone, the blues and greens seeping into a dark gray, into black and white. Everything I knew to be true in the world was now false and cruel. Life lost a bit of its luster and poured from my eyes.

"Don't cry, sweetie," he said.

"You're my daddy," I said.

My dad, a typically reserved man, had opened up at Thanksgiving a couple months prior with a story or two of his childhood adventures. *How long had he known about the tumors? Did he not tell me so it wouldn't sway my decision to move to California? How long did he have?* I don't recall the rest of our conversation, but every desire shifted into a craving for deep connection with him. With this sudden expiration date seemingly stamped across my being, I wanted to bond while I had the chance.

I never found the nerve to ask what time frame or stage the doctors had given. The questions seemed too delicate. I was too delicate and lacked confidence in my ability to handle the answers. My spiritual awakening would grow exponentially when I started to ask myself questions and be honest with the answers. But at twenty-two, much of my life centered around unvoiced questions. The possible answers petrified me.

The next day, I walked into the leasing office at the apartment complex. "I need to transfer my lease to a complex in Dallas," I said. "My dad has cancer."

The vulnerability surprised the leasing consultant and me. Not pausing to wipe the tears, I said, "I'm sorry. It's the first time I've said those words."

She paused. With a wide-eyed, gaping look, she scanned her computer screen in search of the answer for what to do with the crying mess in front of her. I wanted to be held and told that everything would be okay, even if the words registered as fabrication.

"I need to talk to my manager, but I think we can waive any transfer fees," she said.

"How soon?" I asked.

"The process usually requires a month. I think we could probably do it in two weeks."

"Okay," I said. "Okay."

Just as quickly as I'd planned the move to California, I formulated a move back to Texas. I sought comfort from Bradley, who reassured me that moving back was the right choice. Although he blew off several lunch dates before I left, he shipped my car and purchased my flight home. For the second time, and years before the last, he came to my rescue.

Two weeks later, I'd barely unloaded the boxes into my new Dallas apartment before I raced to visit my dad and to right the world by melting into the safety of burly biceps. On the entire two-hour drive to his house, I kept changing the radio station, seeking a place or a song to calm the angst. Every few miles, I'd turn my flashers on and off. I wanted to drive the entire way with my hazard lights flashing, but would rushing to my dad be considered an emergency by anyone but me?

After exiting the interstate for Mt. Pleasant, I rolled through the stop signs and lights until I turned left down the blacktop road that led to his house. Interspersed hay bales lined the hilly road, dotting the pastures of dry grass. A squirrel darted across the road, pausing halfway to turn back in the direction it'd originated. My stomach rose and fell as I accelerated over the mounds, lifting my tush off the edge of the seat before placing me back down, and I recalled the times as a young girl when I'd yelp, "Take roller coaster hill, Daddy."

"You buckled, sweetie?" he'd ask as his foot pressed the gas, giving us the loved thrill.

Minutes later, I pulled into the tree-lined, paved driveway at his home, more or less sliding to a halt as if I'd passed through the finish line ribbon of a car race. Except no cheering crowd clapped nearby, and the only prize to be collected were the fleeting moments of shared time. A sense of urgency grew as life's loud seconds slipped past, which appeared in my mind like the final red seconds on a scoreboard. *Tick*, three. *Tick*, two. *Tick*, one. *Tick*.

I'd sympathized with the thing I knew as cancer—that thing that happened in other people's lives, to other people's families. I lived, however naively, outside its reach in a *"that won't happen to me"* land. But, with the sudden crash into reality, life's fragility connected me on a deeper level of empathy to anyone with a parent gone or dying and to a deeper appreciation for every delicate second.

Guilt metastasized through my body for every time in the past I'd uttered, "I'm so sorry to hear that. Your family will be in my prayers. I heard so-and-so's dad just made a full recovery from the same type," with no visceral understanding of what others were experiencing. I'd nodded my head with a soft reassurance and clasped a friend's soft hand in mine to offer condolences. I wanted to take my hand from the past and slap it hard across my face, leaving only the faint outline of my handprint. But cancer had already done that. Life's sand hourglass flashed across my mind, forcing me into guessing how many granules were left in life with my dad.

With the corner of my shirt, I wiped my face to rid all traces of black mascara trails. My fingertips paused on the chrome door handle as I braced myself for the day I knew would be a life marker, a moment where things would never be the same again. I said goodbye to a life where my dad didn't have a life-threatening illness, painted on a smile, and opened the car door to this new chapter, a life where my dad had cancer.

Looking up to the clouds, something in my core resonated with the drifting puffs. They changed shapes as they passed through space. Did the clouds know what they evolved into before the change? Or did the shift just happen, a surrender to the uncertainty of what the new shape would bring?

My dad's presence spoke the volumes that his mouth never uttered, and I feared not having him in my life. An emotional thunderstorm rolled in, dark and light-battling, and I held onto hope as the world around me was rattled. I hoped for the sunshine after the rain, for the double rainbow, for the happy ending, for the clean bill of health—the peace with the death of his cancer.

Lucky Bob, my dad's orange-ish yellow pound rescue of no known breed, bounced and sniffed across the fresh-mowed green grass in the front yard, indicating my dad must be nearby. Just as Lucky Bob hiked a leg to pee, he noticed my arrival and bounded over to mark his territory on my clean tires instead. I chuckled and scratched him in the sweet spot behind his flappy ears. Lucky Bob never knew just how lucky he was, a last-day save before the shelter meant to euthanize him.

I walked to the edge of the concrete and watched for a moment as my dad tinkered around in the garage shop at the head of the driveway. Creedence Clearwater Revival echoed throughout the metal building from the local classic rock radio station.

He checked a gauge on his Harley before walking to his long, red toolboxes that lined the back shop wall. He grabbed a wrench and wheeled himself underneath his white '97 Dodge Cummins Dually.

Tick, tick.

I braced myself with slow inhales and exhales as I walked closer. Dad had been strong for me through breakups with boyfriends and broken bones and battles with my first stepmother. It was my turn to be strong. I stood next to his truck until he wheeled out on his dolly.

"Well, if it isn't my favorite daughter," he said.

When he stood, I bear hugged him and lingered in the warmth of his farmer-tanned arms. His arms encircled my body, a safety net that momentarily righted the world. The colorful red rose on his left bicep hid another tattoo underneath, and like my father, hid so many secret stories. I didn't know the story of the skull whose place the rose had taken. I'd only been alive for the rose. The skull spoke to experiences before he was my dad, a time before me but that concerned me.

I longed to know all of the stories my dad withheld behind his vaulted lips. My longings for wild—sometimes dangerous—adventures came from somewhere, and my dad seemed to hold their origin behind his closed mouth. His eyes spoke of a knowing, of a life lived, of an unspoken and unprocessed pain. I desperately yearned for him to teach and tell me about his life, thinking that would let me feel more at peace if he passed. The impending loss of another father gnawed at my peace and my ability to live in the present.

Growing up, my mom was so forthcoming with her stories and emotions that it highlighted the fact that my dad rarely disclosed his. His dad, my grandfather, had been murdered when my dad was only fourteen, a secret grief he'd locked away and never processed. As one of the oldest children and with his brother married that same year, the responsibility and pressure to be strong for everyone else had been laid at his feet. He lost his grandfather and his uncle in a plane crash, losing all the men on his dad's side within a span of four or five years. Loss seemed to shadow his life like it later shadowed mine.

The brief snippets I knew of his life kept me hungry. A year or two after his dad died, he'd run away to Montana. He'd ridden bulls, spent nights in jail, and spent years in Germany during the Vietnam War. A six-foot-five and handsome man, I was sure he may have fathered me a sister there. But his wounds led him to a place of inexpression, the same place mine were leading me then.

Like many seem to do after trauma, my dad closed himself off with an invisible emotional barrier around his heart, a defense mechanism to protect himself from pain. But the same wall of his self-protection acted as a divider between us. I craved the depth and openness of a relationship like I once had with Lonnie. I unconsciously modeled him and launched into a civil war with myself, torn between opening my heart to speak and live my truth and drowning or numbing the longing. The thing I wanted most from him was the thing I didn't know if I could give myself.

Equally as stubborn as him and hellbent on getting him to open up, I gave him a book to handwrite memories in, knowing it had always been easier for me to express myself and answer questions with a pen in my hand. As I read the pages of that book now, my soul smiles. When asked what the best thing his dad taught him was, in a cursive blue ink, he wrote, "The best thing was probably trying to be someone he would be proud of."

We not only shared the same wounds; we shared the same longing.

I held him tight, briefly wondered if I hugged him with too much strength. *Was he more delicate now?* I wrapped my arms around his body and continued as if the moment were our last. During our embrace, I didn't want him to think I was treating him differently because of the *C* word. Words I wanted to say formed in little dots above my head as if in a cartoon, but erased just as quickly as the letters formed: *Did the doctors tell how long you had to live? Did they give a time frame?*

I pulled apart and looked into his matching brown eyes, trying to convey in the silence how much he meant to me, how he'd always be the strong man who fixed everything in my life, from cars to hearts. I held his gaze for a few moments before looking through the window at his pet miniature donkeys in the pasture, hoping the silent exchange said more than any words I uttered, giving back what I felt from his eyes.

"How's my favorite daughter doing?" He patted my shoulder with a wink, as if I missed his token joke the first time.

I kissed him on the cheek and said, "I'm your only daughter."

"Still makes ya my favorite. Wanna go for a ride?" he asked, pointing to his Fatboy. "Maybe grab some…"

Before he finished the sentence, I nodded my head like Lucky Bob did when he heard the rattle of the treat bag. I didn't care where we went. I just wanted to go somewhere with him. I gazed at those dark brown eyes that held so much story and smiled as he tightened a worn do-rag over my hair.

"Is this a good look?" I teased, bending down to check the blue and white starred cloth in the side mirror of his motorcycle.

He laughed and gave a thumbs up. He straddled the Harley Davidson—the only true motorcycle, in his opinion—and started the engine. After he eased backwards out of the shop, I stepped on and wrapped my arms around his old beer belly.

As we pulled onto the two-lane highway from the blacktop road, I looked in the tiny side mirror on the motorcycle at the passing pasture. I tossed away the desire to let my mind dance in daydreams of our past memories or in my anxious thoughts of the future, opting instead to enjoy the present moment, the only moment that ever truly exists. Feeling the wind, I leaned into the curve with him as we teetered up to one of the few red lights in town.

"How 'bout ice cream?" he asked when at a complete stop.

"Sure."

Just as the light turned green, he yelled at the car in front of us, "Go! Damn idiots."

I giggled, knowing exactly where I'd inherited my *slight* road rage. We parked at Braum's, the only ice cream shop, and as he retightened the borrowed bandana, he said, "We belong to the Ride to Eat Motorcycle Club versus the Ride or Die MC. We ride the motorcycle to go eat and then we mosey on home."

He chuckled at his own joke again. Our personalities may have been similar in some respects, but we were also as varied as the many options of ice cream displayed in front of us.

"Vanilla?" I said. "But there are so many good flavors...One scoop of cappuccino chunky chocolate and one of mint chocolate chip, please."

"I like what I like," he said, walking to pay for our waffle cones at the register.

Seated across from one another in a comfy maroon, turquoise, and white booth, neither one of us mentioned the *C* word, but its presence lingered in the air like a heavy fog. Pretending his diagnosis wasn't on the forefront of my mind, I smiled and continued licking the cone.

"Shit," he said as a chunk of vanilla ice cream dropped on his shirt.

I hid my smile when he wiped at the small blob with a napkin, only smearing the droplets and leaving little white flecks from the paper cloth on his dark gray shirt. He shrugged and went back to eating his waffle cone.

"So, came to spend time with your dear old dad?"

"Yep," I said.

"Still seein' Grandpa?"

"Dad."

"What? I don't like seeing my little girl get hurt. That's all. And he's too old for you."

I hadn't mentioned anything about Bradley or my feelings being hurt.

"I'm a big girl now and can make my own decisions," I said. "But, no, I'm not."

I left the part out about him being engaged, maybe because a part of me knew he and I would probably get together again, like cappuccino chunky chocolate and mint chip ice cream.

"I want to write a memoir," I blurted.

"A memoir? You're twenty-two. What do you have to write about?" he said.

Why was he doubting me? Anger reddened my face, and I defended my decision with defiance. There was something about my story that mattered, as if the future version of myself were whispering to me in that present moment in the form of my deepest longing. I didn't know how to form the words to tell him that I'd lived and experienced a lot of life that my dad knew nothing about. I hoped he'd be proud, even if some of the details would make him grimace.

His comment about my age registered as doubt in my ability, likely a projection of my own belief. But despite his initial reaction, the following week, he would start forwarding me writing tips and advice emails.

But before leaving the parking lot, he took a picture of me sitting on his steel horse. He held the phone with his arms stretched out, looking down over his nose in search of which button to press.

"It's the circle on the bottom that's not an actual button," I said, finding his technology troubles endearing, recalling the time he'd opened a flip phone expecting to hear a dial tone.

"Ah," he said, nodding and smiling as if he knew it were there the entire time. "Say cheese. Say Harley. Say Motorcycle Mama."

"Motorcycle Mama," I said as he snapped the photo.

I stepped off the bike to let him on and to review the Instagram-worthiness of the picture. With both of us back on the bike, I held the phone out in my hand to take a selfie of us.

"Smile, Pops."

We finished that day without one mention of tumors, doctors, or treatments. Looking back now, I'm glad I hid my anxiety-riddled questions. Even though I aim to be unapologetically myself and speak to the truth of a situation, I'm grateful I quieted the worries and surrendered my urge to control. He deserved a day without talking specifics, a day where he could be my strong father without feeling as if anyone, especially his daughter, may view him as weaker. He deserved at least one more cancer-free day.

*"Love people for who they are and not
for who you want them to be."*

—Alex Elle

11

Less than a month after the move back to Dallas, I was drinking at a bar in Uptown when Chris called.

"I need to come stay with you for a couple of days," he said, a frantic edge to his voice.

"What's up with you?"

Barely able to hear him over the crowd, I walked to the outdoor patio.

"I can't explain on the phone. They're after me," he said.

"Chris, let me call you when I get home. I can barely hear you in the bar. Gonna close my tab now."

Shortly after I walked into my apartment, Colin called me with news that Chris had relapsed and been arrested. Not wanting to believe the news, I searched online. I dropped my phone on the ground after I read, *"Suspect Shoots Up Before Shoot-out at Tyler Apartment."*

I'd later learn that militarized police busted down an apartment door, and Chris, high on meth and believing them to be aliens, had aimed a sawed-off shotgun at the officers and fired.

Not long after his arrest, Chris began calling me collect from jail. Pretty soon, a deep connection and friendship grew between us. With the physical aspect of our relationship removed, a mental connection formed from his full acceptance of every part of me and professed unending love and devotion. Locked away like I was locked away from myself, we awaited his trial, but his chances for freedom looked grim.

I visited him in jail, and although I didn't recognize it at the time, our relationship also fit the mold of an underlying theme for all the men I loved in life. They all were unavailable in some way—emotionally, matrimonially, spatially. There's truth in the lesson that we accept the love we think we deserve, but I hadn't stumbled across that notion or inquired where I'd placed my worth.

At this crossroads of angst and heartbreak, I returned to the home of numbing distractions. Travel, drinks, men, shopping sprees. All flailing grasps for redemption from my own self-rejection.

Chris encouraged me to not put my life on pause, and with Bradley engaged, I devoured other men online from Seeking and Match, one of whom introduced me to a local radio show host, which led to landing an internship with *The Wall Street Shuffle* on KFXR 1190AM. I loved and thrived on creating skits with the producer. On an outing with the show host, I attended an auto show on media day. As I scanned the new vehicle models, people standing next to the vehicles answered questions. Their presence incited curiosity, and an inner question wondered how they had found their jobs. I dismissed the thought, but life would link their jobs and me in a synchronicity several years later.

By late 2011, Bradley sauntered back into my life with just enough time having passed that my memory only recalled the good moments. And although the pain seemed to dominate, it was at least familiar.

After he discovered his fiancée had embezzled over $100,000 from him by ordering on his Neiman Marcus credit card, he had initiated legal proceedings quite different than the ones that typically accompany an engagement. The revelation pleased me. *I would've never stolen from him.* Well, at least nothing more than a razor or hand towel. There's truth in John Ray's words, "Misery loves company"; although now I understand the company to be similar energies riding a lower frequency together.

That fall, after Bradley had booked a European trip with a different young lady, I was standing in my kitchen making breakfast when my phone rang. My heart quickened seeing his name on the screen. I flipped my eggs with a silver spatula and put the call on speakerphone.

"Aren't you with the porn star?"

"She threw a whiskey glass at me from across the bar," said Bradley.

"And you're okay?" I asked. "You sound calm."

"Missed my head by an inch. Glass shattered," he said. "Surprised management let us stay in the hotel."

I'd had a front row seat to how money often pardoned asshole-ish behavior and allowed one to look the other way. I sensed an impending invitation.

"Anyway, I sent her home and don't wanna be a third wheel. I promised this honeymoon trip to my friends. Meet us in Monte Carlo?"

"Shit," I said, as yellow yolk spread across the black frying pan. "Sorry, when?"

"Day after tomorrow? My shopper'll set you up with a Neiman's spree and my assistant will drop off $3,000 for incidentals."

What type of travel incidental could I possibly incur for $3,000 cash? I'll damn sure accept the money though.

While I'd have failed a test to pinpoint Monte Carlo on a map, a quick Google search solved that dilemma, and the town sounded glamorous enough. I didn't like the idea of being anyone's beck-and-call girl, but when beckoned to the French Riviera, subservience became a lot easier to heed. I stamped a veto on feelings of being ever-second choice, the reliable secondhand slippers, and focused on the fact that I'd be traveling to Europe.

I hung up the phone, played Elton John's "Bennie and the Jets," and grooved around my apartment. At the time, my actions and thoughts were bipolar, always swinging back and forth on branches and winds of inner turmoil and uncertainty. What I was *supposed* to be doing in life, what was expected of me, and what I did to please others battled living authentically, embracing spontaneity, and having a good time. Guilt for limited action on my writing matched up against knowing the life experiences would all be pieces of a story. Feeling like an old soul versus realizing I was only twenty-three. Wanting Bradley, and not wanting him. Wanting to not be fully reliant on him but lacking confidence in my ability to survive in a life without him. Beating myself up for indulgence but savoring every ounce of extravagance. Was adventure worth any and all possible heartache and pain? Yes, I believed it was.

I valeted at Neiman Marcus later that evening. Bradley's personal shopper, José, led me to a private dressing area as we raced against closing time.

"Girl, I don't know what he is making up for this time, but Bradley said there was no spending limit," José said.

I love the honest, blunt banter that gay men tend to share with me, like their divulgences carry intel and convey they're on my team. Which felt quite contrary from the straight ones, according to the romantic research I'd conducted up to that point.

"Size six to eight, right?" José asked, turning before I nodded or voiced a yes.

José brought in handfuls of options at a time while soft pop music played in the background. Designer clothes and mink furs lined the walls of the dressing room. Chanel. Missoni. Theory. Helmut Lang. Stella McCartney. Balenciaga. Alexander—Wang and McQueen. Like Julia Roberts in *Pretty Woman*, I was the dress-up doll and these were all of my newfound, stylish friends. Standing in my undies, I ran my hand across the silk, the cashmere, and the suede, falling in love with each graze of my fingertips across the fabric.

Tap, tap, tap. "What's the hold up?" asked José.

"Just a sec," I said, wiggling a pair of black leather pants over my butt.

Pairing the tight pants with a flowy, white, asymmetrical Alexander Wang top and a gray fox fur vest, I stepped out, greeted by José and a coworker he'd brought in for reinforcement.

"1,000 percent. Yes, girl, yes," they said.

He placed a glass of Chardonnay in my hand and pranced across the store with me trailing behind like a power-walking suburbia mom. He stopped to swoop a La Mer skincare set, allowing me a moment to catch up before leading me into a hidden room with racks and racks of furs. Coats of all lengths and shades surrounded us while José went straight to a jacket. "Phew, it's still here. Sometimes they find my hiding spot."

I felt a smidge of guilt thinking of the animal, yet I'd never touched any fabric that soft. Guiding my arms through the coat and facing the mirror, I flipped the black, velvety hood over my blonde head. I flipped the tag over and my eyes bulged at the marked down price of $10,000.

"Aaand, it's reversible...a steal at half off," he said, "I won't let you not take this home."

A steal for $10,000? Well, if he insists.

We wrangled the keepers, racking up close to $20,000 on the Neiman's account.

"Now, shoes," he said.

I trailed José downstairs to the women's shoe area. While slipping into different stilettos and boots, I wondered if I knew which dining fork to use. *I'd have to YouTube that.*

José placed the items on a clothing cart and wheeled the new wardrobe to the valet area to load the items into my car, hugging and kissing my cheeks as he pressed the automatic close button on my trunk.

The following evening, I boarded the flight at DFW airport for London and imagined being a supermodel, carted off to Monaco for a fashion show via a first-class British Airways 777. I slid a new Balenciaga purse, complete with its thick envelope of cash, under the seat in front and stretched my long legs. Shortly after takeoff, the stewardess laid a cloth napkin gently in my lap. Wine washed away my nerves of flying over the sea. I eased into sleep, waking just in time for breakfast service and landing.

Walking alone through Heathrow to catch the connecting flight to Nice, I sauntered with the secret promise of an adventure and daydreamed about where the other travelers were going and why. I loved airports—everyone had a story, always going to or coming from somewhere.

The new Chanel booties stretched tight across my feet, forming a blister on my heel. I tightened my lips and hid a limp on the way to baggage claim. A driver held a handwritten sign: Cristine Bidwell.

Close enough.

After I slid into the back of his SUV, he drove into Monaco and dropped my luggage and me off at a Le Meridien hotel in Monte Carlo. A ripple of panic crept up my spine to greet the jet lag weighing my body into the earth. The crisscross of people buzzing about the lobby incited claustrophobia. The walls of the room inched closer. I pressed on to the front desk.

"Reservation for Jefferies, Bradley Jefferies," I said. "Or Kristin Birdwell."

The French receptionist's eyes widened and responded in faltering English.

"Apologies, no reservation, Miss," she said.

"Maybe Brad Jefferies?"

She typed into her computer screen.

"No, I'm sorry," she replied.

My heart thudded in my throat when my cell failed to gain signal. Bradley and his friends were mid-flight. I tried to recall the name of the correct hotel. *Meta...Meter...No. Fuck, what do I do?*

I winced and wheeled my suitcase next to a pillar, leaning against the round corner column, cursing my feet cemented in the fucking Chanel boots. Tears stung my eyes until an idea flittered to mind. After digging my phone out of the purse, I returned to the front desk and held the device into the air.

"Phone? Could I borrow your phone?" I asked.

I scrolled through my phone contacts to find the number of one of Bradley's assistants. I punched the buttons into the hotel phone and heard an error tone. Frustration seeped out as I attempted again with the country code. When his assistant didn't answer, I left a message, hoping I'd hid the desperation.

My eyelids seemed to need toothpicks to hold them open. I found a quieter corner and perched on top of a suitcase. I'd only been waiting in the hotel for an hour when Bradley ran into the lobby, his neck swiveling in a frantic search, only easing when he spotted me. His arms wrapped around me, holding me with safety and relief.

"Oh, baby," he said.

When I hadn't been at the Hotel Metropole, Bradley sprung into search mode, contacted the driver who'd carted me to the wrong hotel, and found me. His desire for my safety eased us into a cadence for the rest of our week's stay in Monaco, erasing any hesitation I'd felt for our reunion.

The next morning, a spread of breakfast pastries and fruit awaited me in the living area of the suite. His actions were kind and loving, reminiscent of the heartfelt Bradley I'd fallen for in Mexico, the home base for which I'd strived for the last two or three years.

After breakfast on our third morning, the four of us rode in a helicopter for a tour over the French Riviera. Bradley sat in the front while I sat in the back with the newlyweds. The helicopter hovered over the trees, close enough for us to smell the blend of pine. My stomach greeted my throat as the pilot led the whirring machine up and away. Bradley turned to us with a gaping mouth, and we all exchanged looks of wonderment. The ocean kissed the mountains as we glided across the curvaceous shoreline.

When the helicopter landed, we ducked our heads under the whirring blade and jogged to the black SUV. Bradley turned with a contagious exuberance, wrapped his arm around my waist as he kissed my forehead, and said, "First off, that pilot was fucking with us...getting that close to the trees definitely broke code. Second, that thing is like an oversized bumblebee...It ain't supposed to fly."

The helicopter ride was an apt physical representation of our relation-ship, a magical whirring experience that also made me think I may lose my cookies, or marbles, at any moment.

On our last night in Monte Carlo, Bradley and I pranced around the hotel suite in our underwear. He told story after story of his time in college selling weed or of running with the bulls, how he'd give his millions away to turn back time to be my age. This was the Bradley I'd missed, the one so engaged in connecting and sharing his stories. We'd forgotten we'd called room service for fries and stood staring at one another when the doorbell of the suite rang.

"Room service."

"Dare ya to answer the door in your bra and panties," he said.

Without hesitating, I pranced down the long hall. Glancing over my shoulder at him with a grin, he shook his head and a delightful shock registered on his face.

"Hi," I said as I opened the door.

The room service attendant's eyes bulged; a red tint swept over her face, stretching from her décolletage to the top of her forehead. Her eyes darted to the tray in her hands.

"Madame, where should I place the pommes frites?"

I motioned to where Bradley stood in the living room and noticed he'd thrown on a long sleeve shirt and pants in haste. He placed a gener-ous wad of euros in her palm and said, "Merci."

With a prompt nod, she turned to leave, avoiding eye contact on the way out. I tossed the silver covering from the tray onto the coffee table and moaned when the handful of fries met my gaping mouth. Drowning the potatoes in ketchup, I'd missed simple food after a week of decadent dining.

A few hours later, pinks and purples illuminated the sky to announce the promise of a new beginning, a new day. On the balcony terrace, I leaned against the intricate iron railing and stared into the horizon. *Maybe this was a new beginning for us. Bradley turned me to face him.*

"I love you, Kristina Nell Birdwell," he said.

Years of tears streaked down my face upon hearing the words my heart had been longing to hear. "You don't know how long I've waited for you to say those words," I said.

Later that day, I traveled home solo while he continued to Turkey with a business partner and bodyguard. Boarding the plane in a daze, I buzzed after our moment in Monte Carlo. The syllables of the words registered as a promise. Those three words were part of the glue that attached me deeper to him. For a while, I lost myself in translating those words, wondering how that same phrase differed in meaning for two people, how empty words could seem for one when offering life and possibility to another.

The promise of Monte Carlo faded like that winter transitioned into spring. Our relationship seemed as if we were only good for one another when away from home. After the New Year, Bradley fell into a depression cycle and settled into his Dallas home, pining for his lost fiancée and pacifying himself with me. Borderline agoraphobic for the entire next year, he acted as if the world would swallow him up if he distanced himself from his doorstep.

I ached and wanted him to be better to love me fully, without restraint or heartache from his ex-fiancée. If I could overlook his past actions, couldn't he get better for me? Couldn't he live up to who I knew he could be? As he sunk deeper into a depression, I tried to make him happy by saying yes to every late-night sexual request, even if the idea turned me off, turned my stomach, or made me feel less than…like sticking the blunt end of a butter knife into my vagina or giving myself an enema in his bathtub.

I now know people have to choose to help themselves, but for the entire year of 2012, while my efforts seemed fruitless, I damn sure tried. Focusing on Bradley kept me busy, kept my attention off my sick dad, and stalled my focus and actions for my calling.

Around the same time, I started cocktail serving and bartending at the W Hotel's pool. To survive the long shift, I popped Adderall upon waking, not even waiting to brush my teeth before washing the pill down with the water on my nightstand. I equated the stimulants to a strong cup of coffee, only to later calm the energy surge with alcohol. Those little orange pills curbed my appetite, keeping my figure in shape for the bikini uniform, and numbed the feelings of inadequacy.

One evening after a shift and a night out, I woke to a pile of shattered glass shards on the beige carpet at the foot of my bed. I couldn't remember how I'd broken the full-length mirror, but I peered at my reflection as if I'd find the hidden clue to close the gaps in memory. I picked up the edged pieces as if that'd glue my mind back together. I stared, but nothing stared back.

I quit my job by that October, freeing my schedule to escort Bradley to rehab in Sausalito. I flew home solo on the private plane, hopeful about his choice to sober up and hoping for an answer to appear out of the clouds, out of the smoke and mirrors I'd created for myself.

Three days later, when he checked himself out of rehab, the answer appeared—only I didn't listen.

Even though I ached for it, monogamy remained unestablished for both of us. Souvenirs surfaced from some of his conquests: a forgotten pair of panties or a lost lipstick. I neglected to speak my desires, and instead of voicing my wish to be committed, I distracted myself with other men while I waited for him to initiate the deepening of our connection, stuck in a submissive role and dishonoring myself.

*"There is a crack in everything...
that's how the light gets in."*

—Leonard Cohen

12

JANUARY 2013

By the time January rolled around, my inner spark for life had dwindled like a Roman candle sputtering its last shots of fire. Despite my growing resentment toward Bradley with every found souvenir (and toward myself for staying), he and I prepared to venture on a luxurious trip to Paris and Rome with Bob, a father figure of his, and Bradley's assistant, Adam.

I was surprised that he'd committed to the trip since he barely left his house, but I welcomed the adventurous distraction.

One evening during the week leading up to Paris, Bradley and I stood in his large, luxurious bathroom. His blue eyes sparkled as he chopped up lines of cocaine with his black American Express, tapping in promises with every clink of the credit card.

"I'll show you Paris, angel love, and we can discover Rome together," he said. "And we'll show Bob the Vatican."

Bob was a family friend who in many respects had become a father figure to Bradley during his upbringing in the arid desert of West Texas. He admired Bob and wanted to make him proud, something I aimed for with my father. With Bob's recent cancer diagnosis, Bradley hoped to fulfill Bob's long-held wish to see Rome and all of the Catholic wonders.

The tenderness, sentimentality, and support magnetized me to Bradley, drawing me back. Despite all the times he'd yell and throw a cocktail glass against the wall or shut me out when his mood darkened, I hoped he'd allow Paris to be the romantic adventure it could be, or at least take an interest in me outside of the bedroom.

I held my hair to bend forward and inhale the stimulant. After licking my index finger, I ran the red manicured nail along the edge of the glass plate and rubbed a bit of white powder along my gums, enjoying the familiar numbness along my teeth. Bradley's promise would last about as long as the high from the cocaine, but the drugs and booze helped me believe the stories I told myself. *I need him. He'll change. This time will be different.*

I knew there'd be arguments and disappointments. I knew there would be promises broken. I didn't realize then the true value that lies in not breaking the promises made to oneself.

A day after arriving in "the city of love," an unforgiving wind nipped at my skin as Adam, Bob, and I set out to explore. I trudged through the rainy cobblestone streets and buttoned the pleated Burberry trench coat against the crisp air.

We toured the Louvre together while Bradley stayed in his dark hotel room, claiming to be too hungover and sick to join. He would sleep all day, wake late in the afternoon, and drink 'til the early hours of the morning, falling asleep just after sunrise. I pacified myself with the new sights to distract from being ignored by the man I loved.

After walking through the wide hall of an exhibit into an open, expansive space, visitors huddled to one side of the room like moths fighting for a light. As I stood on my tiptoes, Mona Lisa smirked back. I marveled at room upon room of magnificent art and wished I were alone so I could wander for hours.

Adam coached me through my first experience with caviar, smiling as I sipped Veuve Clicquot champagne. Scanning the tiny café, I admired the fashionable couples. Sitting on wicker chairs with wine stands next to the tables, they held themselves with an air of sophistication, enthralled by their own interesting conversations. Even though I emulated the same essence, a part of me felt fraudulent. Champagne and caviar rang a bit incongruous with my country nature. I wondered if the people around us could tell I didn't belong, could hear the long drawl of my southern accent.

"You're up," Adam said.

"Fish eggs, riiiight?" I asked, a little skeptical, but leaning in toward him.

"Mmmhmm, smear some sour cream onto the toast."

"And these little bubbles on top? Here goes nothing," I said.

His grin indicated he got a kick out of my reaction, encouraging my desire to flirt and secure his attention. Rebellious, I still flirted with all of the edges in life and loved attention from older people. I placed the piece of bread into my mouth, nodded my head as I chewed.

"I guess if you like salt, you'll like caviar," I said, tapping my tongue to the roof of my mouth before swishing the dryness away with bubbles.

After Adam signed for the tab, we hit the streets to explore the designer stores with Bradley's credit card. I slipped on a new pair of Dolce & Gabbana denim jeans and lacy, black heels. "What do ya think?" I asked, spinning around in a circle on a raised platform.

Adam rose from the Victorian chair and stepped closer. Scorned by Bradley's choice to stay and drink in the room, I envisioned Adam pressing me back into the boutique dressing room, slamming my back against the wall, and taking me in a moment of passion. I longed for romance and to be desired for more than my appearance, but at the time, physicality was all I gave anyone.

He grabbed the price tag dangling from the back left pocket of the jeans, "I think you've met your limit for today."

"Didn't know I had any," I said.

I stood close to him at the register. The heat from his breath warmed my chest. He moved to grab a bottle of designer cologne for himself, signed the credit card slip, and tossed the bag into the trunk of the large black SUV that waited to give us a driving tour of the city.

An idea sprung to mind when circling around the Arc de Triomphe. I tapped on the driver's right shoulder and pointed my fingers upward to mitigate any language barrier. "Open the sunroof?"

He nodded and the glass slid backwards. The wind whipped hair around my face as I wiggled my head and upper body out of the opening. Bracing myself against the side, I held my phone out to snap a photo. Adam squeezed out the opening and stood in a selfie with me.

My heart battled my mind. With my emotions on a seesaw, my stomach dropped when the Eiffel Tower came into view, emphasizing the emotional distance between Bradley and me. I longed to be experiencing Paris with someone who loved me unconditionally. The type of love displayed between the couples kissing, ones who left locks on the Pont des Arts, an exterior representation of the full acceptance of all the parts of another. Adam stood well in the role of an adventure partner, but I chose to stay away from his fire. Flirting with him was like inching close to warm your backside to a burning flame, yet never facing it to risk being burned.

Wanting to do at least one thing for myself that trip, at my urging, we stopped at Café Procope, the oldest café in Paris. Framed memorabilia lined the red and golden walls, spurring thoughts of all of the famous writers who had worked there. I envisioned myself in the corner working on my own project, steam rising from a hot cappuccino. I'd dip my chocolate croissant into the full cup, savor the deliciousness before wiping a smear of chocolate from my finger to type away on a manuscript. I'd once again yielded to resistance, and my creative desires rested on the back burner. Life seemed easier, more manageable and within my control, when placing my attention and efforts on the wants or needs of others. I had yet to learn that easy or comfortable didn't equate to beautiful.

Later that evening, Bradley joined us for an erotic burlesque show at the Crazy Horse. Limbs fluttered and kicked about the stage, spreading smiles across the audience. Which is why I found it surprising that with both their legs and our spirits high, Bradley tuned in to us at all. Later that evening, he yelled, "You and Adam fuckin'? Did I sponsor this trip for you to fuck my assistant? Pay for some elaborate date?" Then he slammed the door to his adjoining hotel room at the George V.

I curled my hand, raised my fist with fury to pound on the door, but stopped. The sound of ice clanking into a glass and the familiar pop of a liquor bottle top met my ears. The night would only end in shattered glass, slurred words, and hurt feelings. I stood next to the door for a moment, stunned, frozen in time like the ornate art hanging on the wall, blending in like a decoration. Instead of running to Bradley like I typically would have, overcome with a familiar and urgent compulsion to make him happy, to please him, to fix him, I retreated to my bed and picked up the hotel's copy of *The Little Prince* resting on my nightstand.

Something had shifted. After four years of drunken, hurtful outbursts, I didn't want to put up with his shit any longer, as if the sound slapped me across the face with our cyclical behavior. With the slam of the door, an inner angry defiance rose, and I was met with the power to choose my reaction. And although I'd fantasized about sleeping with Adam, Bradley's suggestion of the idea offended me. The words stung, probably because there was that kernel of truth residing in the accusation, but the flirtation was harmless.

After landing in Rome, Bradley booked us separate rooms at Hotel Hassler. For a couple of days, nobody spoke or acknowledged the outburst in Paris and carried on with the trip. He stayed in his room while Adam and I escorted Bob to the Vatican. Our eyes raised to the ceiling, our breath stolen by the intricate detail of the Sistine Chapel. We roamed the hallways of the palace and I imagined myself bathing in Nero's tub. Adam and I eyed one another as we circled the rotundas and zeroed in on our now-firm, unspoken decision to leave one another alone.

In a way, Paris represented where I was, and Rome hinted at where I could be. Rome exuded joy and warmth, a stark contrast from the dreary and sad Paris I'd experienced. Rome's history and architecture told stories. As I toured the ancient Colosseum, in my mind's eye gladiators fought one another as crowds erupted into chants. I didn't know then that I carried a heavy shield as well, and that to heal, I'd have to shed my armor. That I'd built a coliseum around my heart only to tear it down brick by brick years later. That my happiness wouldn't be found in the chanting crowds, but by the brave woman in the ring.

Pizza and limoncellos fueled a round of shopping at leather shoe boutiques and Prada until we returned to the hotel, exhausted from the weight of shopping bags. The only thing Bradley explored was the bottom of a Crown Royal bottle in his hotel room. Although distracted by all the newness, I couldn't comprehend why he skipped out on the main reason for this trip. I'd accepted his belittlement of me, but to Bob, an adored father figure? Having grown fond of Bob myself, Bradley's actions registered as the ultimate betrayal.

He joined us for dinner that evening in Rome. I'd barely cut into a plate of foie gras when he placed his crumpled black napkin on the table and stood. "We're leaving tomorrow," he said, broadcasting the decision without discussion in a "because I said so" manner.

After nine days, jilted by Bradley's desire to leave early before spending any meaningful time alone together, I rushed down the Spanish steps and cut down a side street while tears washed down my cheeks. Copper and nickel coins glittered across the base of the Trevi Fountain. Not knowing what to wish for and only wanting to drown my emotions, I vowed to not attempt to clear the air. Bradley hadn't shown me the city, only that he was incapable of change. And I had stayed around hoping for him to, clinging to my idea of his greatness.

The next day, we departed Rome to switch planes in Paris for a direct private flight to Dallas. With maroon reader glasses perched at the end of his nose, Bradley turned the pages of a newspaper while he smoked a cigarette and blew the smoke toward the open, tinted window of the black suburban. Now and then, I glanced from the streets of Paris to see if he'd make eye contact, to see if he'd acknowledge the argument, the space between us, or maybe even just me, but his eyes never drifted from the black and white pages.

I longed to be separate from him, separate from anyone else wanting me to be someone I wasn't, including myself. A part of me wanted to rip the newspaper out of his hands and yell with hands shaking in rage, *Don't you remember your promise? The "I'll show you Paris and we can discover Rome together" promise?*

When the chauffeur arrived at the tiny FBO, the fixed-base operator, where our private plane was to depart, an assistant carried my bags onto the Falcon jet. I walked up the steps wearing gold, oversized Tom Ford sunglasses and a red Prada purse on my forearm. Taking off my gray fur vest, I placed it on the adjacent open seat as if to signal the space as taken. At the front of the plane, a map on the screen outlined the nine-hour journey to Dallas. Nine long hours.

I unbuckled and went to the restroom. Pulling one of my favorite pills out of my pocket, I popped the Xanax in my mouth.

Since my dad's cancer diagnosis two years prior, I'd grown accustomed to numbing my feelings with alcohol, pills, cocaine, men. I didn't know then that selectively numbing only the bad emotions wasn't an option. I numbed them all, even the great ones. My reflexive reach for the pill container had quickened, and I found myself rationalizing the consumption. *It's for my fear of flying.* And oh, how I flew. I fled and flittered about to men, substances, and experiences outside of myself in an unending search. Yet how could I stop the hamster wheel I didn't even know I was on?

I flushed to seem like I had used the restroom and applied lipstick before returning to my seat. The flight attendant placed a cocktail napkin on a ledge next to the window and a small vase of pink and red roses. "Champagne before take-off, miss?"

I nodded. I fondled the pink roses nestled in the cupholder, drinking small sips from the glass and scratching at the coral stain of lipstick with my thumb until the painted vertical lines smeared. As the plane passed through clouds on our ascent, thoughts drifted to the surface before the pseudo-peace of Xanax warmed my body and converted the anxious, incessant stream of discontent into words of reasoning.

Why did I cling to Bradley? When his words bit at my being and ripped against what remained of my self-respect, why did I not voice my feelings? Why did I stay? For four years, I'd accepted the other women from the sugar daddy website despite longing for monogamy, despite my inability to trust what he, or any man for that matter, promised, and despite my own philandering behavior.

I now know I endured the years of verbal abuse because I didn't believe I deserved better treatment and thought the lifestyle was worth the pain. The lies and masks I presented to everyone else rested on the largest ones I told myself. Resentment had soured the love I had for Bradley, and although I didn't have the verbiage or awareness then, I'd grown accustomed to poor treatment by neglecting my truest inner desire to write, to follow my heart, and to be free. I felt stuck living in what I now understand as the outer reflection of inner unresolved traumas and unconscious patterning.

Bradley said he'd always be there—if in no other way, at least financially. I lacked trust in my ability to survive on my own, to leave the security blanket of Bradley's wire transfers to my bank account despite the blanket's worn, frazzled texture weighing against the fiber of my soul. Disconnected, my silenced desires harbored me within inauthenticity and stroked my ego in "achieving" the lack of belief in myself. By playing small and safe, I proved my fears right. As a woman and child of the '80s and '90s, conditioned to behave and obey, to be nice and obedient, I hadn't learned to listen to myself. I hadn't learned to love my wild reckoning with the world. I had never learned to choose myself.

The plane dinged, alerting us that we'd reached 10,000 feet. I unbuckled and laid down on the queen-sized bed at the rear, melting into the sheets with the soothing effects of the benzo coursing through my system.

When we landed in Dallas, restlessness descended over me again. Despite spending ten days exploring two European cities I'd dreamt of visiting, unease seemed to be my only souvenir. Although I presented a happy disposition, a depressive cloud shielded true joy. Somehow through the pill fog, an inner knowing told me I had to do something. I didn't know what or how, and I felt lost between points of destinations that I couldn't quite define.

That same evening, a black town car drove me to my apartment in Uptown Dallas. I scanned the desolate hallway, shivered at its similarity to The Shining, and hastily unlocked my apartment door. I rolled my silver Tumi suitcases into my walk-in closet and slid down against the wall.

From outward appearances, I owned every*thing* I wanted and went on lavish vacations. If I had every*thing* I wanted, why wasn't I happy? Looking around the closet, a realization hit: accumulating more and more designer things pushed me further away from myself and upped the dose needed for pacification.

None of this shit matters. Not the jewelry adorning the dresser. Not the designer clothes hanging on the racks. Not a single materialistic item. Not a damn one.

I sat with the realization before recognizing that presenting perfection had been my aim my entire life. And if what I'd known, believed, and chased weren't true, then what in the hell was the truth? I thought of Bradley, and at that moment, I understood money wasn't a cure-all—the richest person in my life was also the most depressed. A chill ran down my spine and the closet seemed to close in, encircling my life choices with loneliness.

I'd typically found solace in spending time alone because I didn't have to be anyone else with myself. But, at that moment, I felt foreign to myself, dark and lonely instead of alone. Why stay in Bradley's orbit? If my wings fluttered away from his nest, would I fall to the ground?

I thought about walking out of the closet and pretending that realization had never come, but I knew there'd never be an unknowing. I could alter the trajectory with different actions, say goodbyes for new hellos. I thought about how I'd read once that it was better to try and fail at the life you truly wanted than to succeed at a life you despise. So which pain did I want—the pain of pursuit or the pain of warped practicality?

The emotion started at a deep pit in my stomach and worked its way up my throat. The sound first escaped my mouth as a gasp before turning into a sob. It was as if my body knew what I didn't consciously think about then. I'd have to grieve a version of myself, a version I'd once loved.

When I woke the next morning, I longed to curl right back under the covers and stay in bed all day, to have my biggest exertion be answering the door for pizza delivery. Not only was I jet-lagged, but I was also tired. Tired of people-pleasing, tired of pretending to like or do things, tired of not doing what I wanted. I'd abandoned myself, trying to make everyone else happy in an unconscious attempt to manipulate their actions into not abandoning me. But what about me? I wanted to be me.

I wanted to be happy. I'd contorted myself to become some ideal candidate for marriage, to be safe and secure, even though a typical marriage wasn't what I wanted. Why?

I put my needs and wants on hold to be the perfect friend, to be the perfect lover, to be loved and adored. I'd molded myself into what I thought everyone else wanted for so long, I didn't know who I was.

I rolled out of bed and slipped into a black, silky robe. I splashed water on my face and looked at the scattered pill containers on the counter. I brushed my teeth and glanced at the closet door, recalling the experience behind the white frame. *Did I have the courage?*

The little girl who believed she could be and do anything whispered, but as an adult I questioned: *could I make it on my own?* A part of me remembered that rebellious, spunky girl. But was I the same girl who used to examine her six-millimeter-gap buck teeth in the mirror? Who spewed water at her brother from the space between those two teeth? The tomboy who knew no fear, or at least never allowed her life to be dictated by it? Who knew she could be and do anything that she wanted?

How did I go from her to here?

Who am I? What do I want? Why am I here?

Am I even worthy enough to be asking these questions?

"For we have to learn the art of enjoying things because they are impermanent."

—Alan Watts

13

FEBRUARY 2013

On a Sunday afternoon that February, I visited my dad at his home. Over the last two years, amidst all the pining for Bradley and the partying, I'd made frequent trips to spend time with my dad, both at his home and at the various hospitals he frequented for his cancer treatments. I lived for the promising moments after a doctor's words offered hope and encouragement. But for this trip, instead of focusing on encouragement for his health, I needed encouragement for myself. I didn't know if he'd be able to offer that, but I was willing to see.

After arriving at his home, I found my dad in the living room seated in his trusty recliner. He peered over his reading glasses, finding and pecking the keys on the computer while chuckling at a blog called "Angry White Man." Walking past the brick fireplace, I sat on his lap and hugged him.

"Still not smoking, are ya?" I asked.

"There may have been a few...slips," he said.

"Hiding them again?"

He glanced to the top of the fireplace, out of reach and sight from my stepmother, where a pack of cigarettes rested on its side.

"Dad, I've been thinking about moving back to California," I said. "Something is telling me I need to be there, maybe take some classes."

"Kristin, sometimes you have to do what makes you happy...and quit worryin' about making everyone else happy," he said.

My tension melted upon hearing those words—the best advice he'd ever given me—and I decided right there and then to move back to Los Angeles. The comment was a blessing for my decision, which alleviated guilt from feeling like I was leaving my dad too soon in his battle with cancer. When I moved the first time, he'd expressed how he'd never see his little girl, but this time around, he uttered no words of disapproval.

Within a couple weeks, I'd sold furniture and packed my clothes and memorabilia into my car, playing Tetris with my belongings and donating anything that didn't fit with this newfound craving for simplicity. My dad continued forwarding emails on the writing process and at lunch on the day before I drove west, he handed me an atlas and an embroidered pillow: *Always live the life you love.*

"Just in case you get lost," he'd said.

Bradley and I hadn't spoken since returning home from Europe, and for about a month after my move, I stayed with a friend in

Valencia while interviewing for different jobs in the heart of Los Angeles. This time around, I seized opportunities with renewed vigor. The Universe felt as if she were working with me to align my future. I signed up for a writing class through UCLA Extension and found two jobs within a couple of weeks. Even though they weren't my ideal jobs—an internship with an online Jewish news website and a bartender gig in West Hollywood—I believed they would lead to or bring me closer to the ideal.

With a renewed fervor, I created a vision board and placed *"I love my new apartment by the ocean"* on the black surface with a magnet. I'd look at the board and hear the sound of the ocean, feel the peace in its proximity. Without a doubt, I knew I'd be living near the beach. There was no alternative. I have a deeper understanding today about the physics behind manifestation—how raising our vibration to match our desires with good thoughts and gratitude and taking aligned action, like saying yes to new opportunities, leads to a desire's fulfillment. Instead of forcing or controlling, I flowed with life, acted on intuition, and didn't second-guess myself. I trusted in the support of the Universe without fully grasping the methodology or science behind what I was doing. I went with what made sense, what resonated, and watered the quantum physics seeds Lonnie planted years prior.

When I stumbled across a Craigslist advertisement for a beach apartment, I wasn't surprised when the manager said I'd be the first to view the studio inside the older, stucco residential building. I peered around the edge of its tiny balcony to see the sand less than fifty feet away. I crossed my fingers and hoped my energy would help with my lack of stable employment history. The friend I lived with owned a landscaping company and allowed me to lie on the application and say I worked

for him. I had the money, the credit score, and the employment alibi...
nothing was going to get in my way.

Once I'd moved in, I spent the mornings walking to a café and eaves-
dropping on neighborhood conversations while I ate breakfast and
worked on blog posts or screenplay ideas. With earbuds in and no music
playing, aiming for incognito, I listened for any clever lines to borrow
for a project. Then at night, I'd slide the window above my bed open
and listen to the waves break onto the shore. I visited the farmers mar-
ket, fell in love with Harry's Berries, and settled into my new home. Life
appeared to be on an upswing.

Less than a month after returning to California and a week after
moving into the new apartment, my dad's mom, Nana, called. "You
may want to come home soon, Kristin."

"What's 'soon'? A week from now, a month, tomorrow?" I asked.

"Well, Tommy isn't eating or drinking anything," she said. "Had an
Ensure a day ago."

The blood drained from my limbs, and I collapsed onto the bed. The
news didn't make sense. A couple days prior, I'd chatted with him about
bringing his Harley to California and riding up Pacific Coast Highway
together. He'd been placed on hospice, but he told me his hospice wasn't
a death sentence. I knew hospice to be end-of-life care, but I had believed
him. I know now that our desire to believe something can supersede the
truth staring us in the face.

I'd finally felt as if life were meeting me halfway, ironically enough,
when I met it halfway. My spirits and resolve faltered after her call,
and I called the person I relied on in any moment of crisis: Bradley.
"I...I need to go home to say goodbye to my dad," I said, my voice
quavering.

"Oh, baby. Is this a charter situation or can you take the first flight out in the morning?"

"My Nana said soon, I don't know what soon means. Tomorrow morning, I guess?"

Bradley called the Centurion travel concierge and booked a ticket to Dallas. And while I craved the comfort of his arms or to hear words of reassurance, for him to let me know everything would be okay, he rescued me for the third time.

I emailed my writing instructor about my absence and went through the motions of packing my suitcase, pressing the folded clothes into their place. I zipped my toiletry bag. I'd braced myself for this moment since his diagnosis. Two years, and I still didn't feel prepared. No amount of preparation could have braced me for the pain, despair, grief, anger, and abandonment I'd soon experience.

The chipper flight attendants triggered the little girl inside and stirred a tantrum of frustration and anger on the plane ride. *Don't they know I'm flying to say goodbye to my dad?*

I landed at DFW just shy of noon on April 13, 2013. In Bradley's pre-arranged rental car, I sped along the interstate with the emergency flashers on while the growing pit in my stomach assumed the worst on the two-hour drive to my dad's house. *Not yet, Daddy. Please, not yet.*

I parked among the numerous familiar vehicles filling the driveway. Nana, my brother, my aunts and uncle. How had I not known his health was this bad? Why didn't anyone tell me anything? Walking through the front door, I pushed my sunglasses on top of my head, revealing my tear-stained face.

"Tommy, Kristin's here," said Nana. "She came all the way from California to see you."

The crowd clumped together on the sectional couch in my father's living room, around the brown La-Z-Boy recliner where he rested in an unresponsive, sleep-like state.

"Don't remember him like this," said my Uncle Bill.

I nodded and pleaded with my eyes for everyone to leave the room. I sat on the edge of the recliner next to photo albums spread out on the coffee table like shuffled poker cards, telling the story of Dad's gamble with life. In that limbo moment, just before one of us folded, I believed he and I held losing hands—not knowing the game is rigged for us all to win, if only we learn and grow with each passing round.

With every inhale, the air rattled his lungs and announced death's approach. Silent tears streamed down my face as my hand clutched his clammy palm.

"Hey, Daddy," I said.

He didn't respond.

"You know you're my favorite dad in the whole world, right?"

For a brief moment of recognition, his eyes met mine and his lips formed a faint rendition of his token, goofy smile before falling back into his rattled slumber. I looked around the empty room for my courage. I needed to give him the reassurance; I needed to give it to myself as well.

"It's okay, Daddy. I'll be okay. I love you. Go."

His bony arm jutted through his gray shirt. *When had he gotten so thin?* This frail man wasn't how I wanted to remember my dad. I wanted to remember the strong dad, the man who fixed everything. I kissed his forehead and moved to the adjacent couch.

Picking up one of the worn photo albums splayed across the coffee table, I browsed through glimpses of another era. I traced my index finger over a picture of my mom wearing wide sunglasses while sitting on his lap. The photo directly below showed him wearing the same sunglasses, reflecting a distant time when they were in love. A tear fell on a youthful me, bent over his lap receiving birthday spankings. Then, on a Polaroid showing a slender version of my dad standing next to a motorcycle in Germany, where he'd worked as a medic in the army. The military photo spurred a memory of a conversation we'd had at the veterans' hospital after his first treatment.

"At least the VA is paying for everything," I had said.

"Yeah, but if it weren't for the army, I probably wouldn't be in this position."

I'd stared out the window into the parking lot. A bit woozy from the morphine, he continued, "You could be a nurse, like Miss Jay over here."

"I've already graduated, Dad," I had said.

Needing fresh air, I greeted my mom on the front lawn. As soon as she embraced me, the sobs that'd been waiting to escape released. With one parent on the brink of death, I needed the comfort of her presence more than anything.

"Whatshername, your stepmom, Ann, met me at the front door and didn't want me to come inside," my mom said.

"I don't care what she says. He's the father of your children...I need you right now."

"I know, babe, but this is her house. I told her I was here for you guys, but part of me wants to say something to him too, ya know?" she said.

"You have every right to," I said.

"I kept hoping for a miracle. This just makes it final; we're never going to get back together. If there was any man to get back with, it was your dad. And I probably shouldn't even tell you that."

"It's okay," I said.

Our roles switched for a moment, and I comforted her in my arms as she cried.

Everyone left at dusk except my Nana, my stepmom, and me, opting to stay the night at my dad's house and sleep with Nana in one of the spare bedrooms. At 3:00 a.m., I woke. I tiptoed into the living room to listen to my dad. His breath shook down the hallway. I never expected to be comforted by the sound of approaching death, but the sound meant he was still with me. I went back to bed, and at 5:05 a.m., my stepmom shook my shoulders.

"Kristin, he's gone. He's gone," she said.

I walked between the living room and the kitchen area, trying to out-pace the guilt from the brief feeling of relief in his passing. He was no longer in pain. I tried not to look at the body of my father in his recliner, leaning back with his mouth and eyes open, but every now and then, I couldn't help but steal a glance at the painful reality. I worked up the nerve to say goodbye one final time. I kissed his cold forehead and closed his eyes. Grabbing my phone and earbuds, I ran outside, down the drive-way, and onto the paved black top county road. I ran and ran until the pavement turned into gravel, until the gravel turned into pasture.

The outside reflected my inner emotions, as everything I ran past was a blur. The world came back into focus when I slowed to a walk. No matter how fast or where I went, I couldn't escape the fact that he was gone. And even though I knew he'd died and hadn't departed by choice, I felt he'd left me.

A few people drove past me, probably just another normal day on their way to work. *I just need a sign, Daddy. Anything. Let me know I'm not alone.* I knew he wasn't in pain anymore, but I wanted to be selfish then. *I lied, Daddy, I'm not okay.* I wanted him back. I wanted to hug him just one more time, to feel those burly arms around me once more. With my thumb, I hit shuffle on the iTunes songs on my phone. I couldn't believe my ears when our favorite Eagles song, "Seven Bridges Road," popped up to play first.

Seven years later, I would read a book about signs from loved ones. I can now see this was his first time communicating after death. But in that moment, I hit play and bawled to the perfect, five-part harmony.

When I arrived back at the house, my stepmom had gone to the hospital complaining of chest pains. I waited with my Nana for the hospice nurse and the funeral home to arrive to come carry his body away.

"I can't be in here," said Nana.

"I understand," I said as she walked down the hall to the back bedroom. I didn't want to be in the room either, but I'd somehow been volunteered to be the strong one for everybody else.

My dad's pain medicine and Xanax bottles rested on the counter in the kitchen. I shook some of the Vicodin and Xanax into my hand, making sure to leave enough pills to avoid any suspicion. The hospice nurse arrived a few moments later and disposed of the rest of the medication.

"Is this everything?" she asked.

"Yeah," I said, glad I'd swiped the meds when I did and wishing I'd taken more.

They loaded my dad in a body bag and onto a stretcher. Seeing him carried away was too much to handle. Each step they took with my dad placed me further into a well of sorrow and abandonment. And I didn't want to do it sober.

I hugged my Nana and walked outside. Standing outside, I tossed a couple pills into my mouth. With a swig of water, I washed them down and said goodbye to a life with my dad in it and said hello to a life without him. I washed down the guilt from brief moments of gratitude that he was no longer in pain and opened the door of my dad's dually truck. Sitting in the driver's seat, I picked up his pack of Marlboro Reds and lit one. Smoking one of his cigarettes was as poetic as I believed it'd be—for all of about two minutes, before I started hacking and coughing. Then I laughed, thinking I'd coughed on the ghost of him because he never wanted me to smoke.

After we'd buried his ashes next to his father in Coleman, Texas, seeping rage sat beneath my skin, silently building and begging for attention. My cycle of feeling abandoned and in turn abandoning myself turned into a self-pity, amplified by grief, that built to anger by the time I made it home to Venice after the funeral. Now a hermit and out of pills, I ghosted my jobs and piled my oily hair on top of my head into a messy knot. I shuffled from the bed to the bathroom and back to the bed, from the fridge to the bed, from the door for delivery to the bed, from the fridge to the bed. At night, I slid the window above my bed open and let the lullaby of the sea soothe me to sleep.

For a split second in the morning, I'd wake closer to joy, having forgotten he was gone until the agony begged and punched my pillow. *Why did you leave me so soon?* I reasoned there must be something I was supposed to take away from his death. There had to be a reason why he was taken from me at twenty-four, why he died at only fifty-nine. *What purpose could this feeling of abandonment and darkness serve in my life?*

My mom once told me that when one door closes, another opens, but life just may be hell in the hallway for a bit. A moment from childhood sprung to mind. When I was eight or maybe nine, I'd approached my mom outside of our house before one of her evening walks. Craving her

158

attention now that she was home from work, I tugged at her nerves and the lower portion of her faded, oversized cotton T-shirt and asked if I could walk with her. She shushed me and told me she had to be alone to talk with God.

I no longer believed in the God I grew up with. Maybe in something bigger than myself, or something I couldn't put my finger on, but the name "God" stirred judgment and registered as another disappointing man in my life. But after I arrived home near the healing ocean waters, I decided to take walks with my dad and talk to him in my journal afterwards. I vowed to get out of my bed as many days as possible and wander along the Venice shore. I needed a healing mission to peel myself out of bed and to get myself into the hallway.

Journal Entry: Sunday, April 21, 2013—12:25 p.m.

Dear Dad,

It was overcast on my walk today. I like it when the weather matches my mood. No sun, but bright enough to still wear sunglasses. The shades also shield the tears from the strangers. It just makes more sense to cry when it's overcast.

I walked closer to the edge where the sand is more packed. With one iPod bud in my ear and the other free with the sound of the ocean, I felt as if my hearing was similar to yours. "Sit on my good side," you would say.

I used to mouth words and not say anything at all in your good ear, but you never knew when I was joking. Was your deaf ear like constantly having the ocean in that ear? That doesn't seem so bad.

A father chased a little girl on the sand. The girl giggled until he finally captured and lifted her in the air. Memories flooded in of you chasing me around the front yard of our yellow house. I never understood how you caught me every time. It was unfathomable for me to think that you could actually be faster than me.

I hate to say it, but this emotional pain feels like the hardest breakup I've ever experienced. From the one man I thought could never break my heart.

Until tomorrow.

Journal Entry: Thursday, April 25, 2013—3:00 p.m.

Today has been especially hard for me. I glanced at my favorites on my phone and saw your name still sitting at the top of the list. As much as it kills me, I listen to a saved voicemail just to hear your voice. Over and over.

Mom told me that as hard as the pain is to experience, it is healing to feel the feelings. I sure as hell hope so. It's crazy to me how vast the feelings are from day to day. I miss you.

Journal Entry: Thursday, May 2, 2013—9:45 a.m.

I hadn't anticipated feeling sad on my birthday. But it is my first one without you.

A year ago today, I received the best gift from you, a book of handwritten stories and memories after you completed the book of "homework" memories I gave you. "I don't know what I did to deserve two great kids," you wrote. Well, I don't know what I did to deserve such a great dad who taught me valuable life lessons:

- That you can sometimes say more with one look than any words.
- That Confucius said, "One degree equals two happy parents."
- That a happy biker can be identified by the number of bugs in his teeth.
- That life isn't about the destination, it's about the scenic route.
- That life shouldn't be taken so seriously.
- That in a pinch while camping, you can take a bar of soap to the lake.
- That a perfect day is good weather with friends and family.
- That we only get one shot at this ride of life, make the most of it.

Thank you for an amazing twenty-four years.

Initially, I interpreted my dad withholding his true health from me as a display of his innate stubbornness, but I now feel the love in his actions. Cancer-ridden, death knocking, knowing all too well the pain of losing a father, he'd acted from a place of love, in an effort to protect the emotional well-being of his children.

My soul started speaking louder through this vessel of deep pain and depression, howling at me like a wolf until overcome with an insatiable desire to feel whole and worthy, searching for the peace in freedom and telling my story. The overwhelming inner agony of being the version of me I knew others loved, but not being me for myself, drove me to find the courage for authenticity and to love myself.

The next seven years of my journey would teach me how to find the gifts of grief, in the loss of our loved ones and in the death of our former selves, and how to live a life I loved. While I believe our entire story makes up our journey, losing my dad was a pivotal moment that propelled me on a healing, spiritual quest to answer my inner questions, to speak my truth, to live with purpose, and to step forward into love and trust.

But not without at least one more detour.

"The phoenix must burn to emerge."

—Janet Fitch

14

uring the immediate months after my dad's death in 2013, I'd resolved to a new normal, a new emotional baseline of emptiness and despair, with the occasional visit from anger and abandonment. I'd check in with myself, and Google on occasion, to see where I landed on the spectrum of grief stages, to see if I was headed in the right direction. I wanted to feel better, but I couldn't seem to motivate myself to do anything, stuck in a cyclical pattern of eating, Netflix, and sleeping.

Guilt mounted from my summer of binge-watching TV in bed. Feeling true, lasting joy again seemed impossible. I'd come to terms with the notion that I'd never feel exuberance again in a life without my dad. An excellent pretender to any friends or family interested in my well-being, I wore a façade and kept my emotions together for other people. *Oh, yeah, California is going great. I love living by the beach. Time of my life. Land of dreams.* By feeding the energy of loss, my existence felt hollow. An existence of emptiness radiated back to me with each click of the Apple TV remote. Panic arose every time I lost the silver remote of solace in my tousled white sheets.

My higher self wanted to heal one way or another; my subconscious started processing the loss with repeated lucid dreams. I would have a dream that my dad was tickling my feet, and then wake up because my body felt like someone was in my apartment rubbing their fingers along my bare soles.

With a conscious awareness despite meeting in a dream, I would tell him, "You're not supposed to be here."

"Shhh, don't tell anyone," he'd say with a smile.

In the middle of one summer evening, hours after Netflix prompted, *Are you still watching?*, I jolted awake in my apartment. My eyes opened wide and the hair all over my body stood at attention. Every muscle tensed as my heart thudded with an awareness that someone else was in the room with me. Without moving my body, an effort to not alert the intruder, I slid my gaze to the area where the slender hallway met the gas fireplace. My eyes met a six-foot-five golden, shimmering apparition.

I squished my eyes a few times and stared at the smooth ceiling. No doubt the energetic presence was my dad. I'd traded pills and booze for binge watching TV, my bare stomach acting as a table for snacks. I may have been numbing my emotions with new methods, but I was the most sober I'd been in my life since I was a child. Well-rested. Hydrated. Even vegan at the time. Despite the overwhelming grief, I felt sane. Yet I no doubt sensed a palpable presence in my studio that evening. I couldn't deny its existence or discredit the experience. But how was that possible?

Looking back, I feel as if my dad wanted me to have a visual understanding of the fact that he never abandoned me, that he just wasn't limited to the physical form that had once brought immense comfort. He'd found a way to communicate the message that he was okay. The visit helped me get out of bed and press play on life.

The mountain of healing ahead seemed insurmountable. But like riding my mountain bike today, a hill appears more daunting from a distance. In the space between, intimidation can build to the point where I almost want to turn around before trying. But if I place one pedal down and then the other, no matter how slow I go, I'll make it to the top and ride on the other side. The golden apparition was the match to my spiritual fire and gave me the resolve to get back on my bike and keep pedaling.

My inner question shifted—from seeking the answers to desperate pleas of *Why me, why did my dad leave me so early*—closer to an understanding that maybe I was experiencing this pain because I was strong enough to handle it. *What was this trying to teach me?* Maybe I could mold the grief into something beautiful, a transference of energy similar to what happened with death, and give myself a new life, a life of my own.

Much of life comes down to perspective. With this new outlook, I craved knowledge and understanding. I read book after book, and notably picked up *The Artist's Way* by Julia Cameron. With each finished chapter and exercise, I progressed on a journey from victimization to empowerment.

The Artist's Way helped nurture my artist, and my inner child, to heal and to create. In addition to my stream-of-conscious journaling "morning pages," the workbook nudged me to explore my longings. I enrolled in an acting class to step toward my storytelling dream, figuring it'd also help get me out of the house at least twice a week.

During this time, a writer and former classmate at UCLA Extension inspired me to pay closer attention to the details of my life by taking note and being grateful for the people, things, and experiences in my day-to-day. I jotted down moments or things I came across, however large or small, that incited a sense of appreciation, wonder, or insight. I kept a running tab in a note in my phone that evolved to become a gratitude scrapbook of sorts. The notes grew into a regular gratitude practice where I'd post the month's moments on my blog.

I'd quit both of my jobs after my dad died, but Bradley continued to wire money into my account while giving me space for a year. Instead of partying and shopping, I used his money as an investment, channeling the funds into my healing and my dream. Maybe it was how I felt my previous pain entitled me to it, or seeing him reciprocate the help I had given his wounded self for years, or the switch in my own narrative— whatever the reason, I had no qualms accepting his money.

Less than six months after my dad died, in the tight hallway of a Meisner-based acting studio in Santa Monica, I stood with my ear tilted toward a white door, waiting for a break in the class scene to return. A beautiful brunette woman smiled as she joined me from the hallway restroom. Her soulful brown eyes looked into mine. She held depth behind them, and her energy sparked my curiosity. She was from Azerbaijan and a fellow writer.

My soul lit up at meeting Tahmina, a woman with shared long-ings. She quickly became my closest friend and writing partner in Los

Angeles. Over the course of the next year, she helped me smile and feel joy again. We'd meet at a new restaurant, gorge on the food, and discuss our insights on life, spirituality, and creativity. We encouraged one another to shine, and in February of 2014, we attended a seminar led by Bob Proctor, one of the thought leaders from *The Secret*, a documentary I'd loved since my mom had introduced me to it in high school.

One afternoon over coffee, we shared disappointments over the movie industry and concluded that since we hadn't received our desired opportunities, we'd create our own. One evening at her oceanside Malibu apartment, brainstorming ideas over pizza, she asked, "What about a movie that displays both of the worlds we are from?"

"Will you hand me the crushed red pepper?" I said. "And I love that idea—incorporates our story and will be natural for us to portray."

"Maybe a man choosing between staying in his comfort zone or living outside of it?"

"Mmm, what about a dying man reflecting back on his life?" I asked.

"*Ooh*, the two great lost loves of his life," she said.

Our eyes lit up. "Yes!"

Having settled on an idea, we next settled on the carpet on her living room floor, meditated, and surrendered any remaining frustrations to the tide.

In the spring of 2014, after co-writing *The Last Recollection* about a dying man recollecting on the two great and dynamically different loves of his life, Tahmina and I raised $8,000 on Kickstarter, hired a production company, held auditions, and filmed the short over three days.

While shooting a beach montage scene of the younger version of the old man and my character, dolphins greeted us from the water, leaping out of the water and into our footage. Driving away from the Malibu beach, I instinctively picked up my phone in an urge to call my dad and relay my excitement to him. A wave of sadness washed over me, but almost as quickly, the same presence from my apartment encompassed me and instilled an immediate understanding that somehow, he knew.

Space breeds insight because I have a clear understanding that there was also a part of me then that felt guilt for feeling joy again. A part of me felt unworthy, wanting to cling to the story that had let me live in the pain and suffering. A part of me had become addicted to feeling victimized, as if I could only allow myself a certain amount of happiness and needed to remain sad and withdrawn to prove the love I held for my dad. At the time, my pain seemed like the only remaining thread connecting me to the warm tapestry of him. These beliefs left me vulnerable to self-sabotage.

By this point, Chris's mom Lori had evolved to become a second mother. I idolized her ability to be unapologetic with her life and interactions, even when some of the behaviors were self-destructive. She claimed her story. She was one of the least judgmental people, owning up to her mistakes while making you laugh over jokes about her own questionable decisions, once telling me the only thing she was allergic to was hypocrisy. Her heart remained kind, untarnished by bitterness, despite experiencing gut-wrenching abuse. She introduced me to Marianne Williamson, an author and spiritual teacher, and thanked me for loving both versions of her—Sober Lori and Pill Lori—which was reciprocal. Together, we mourned the loss of the freedom of her son, who had agreed to a plea bargain for a life sentence in prison a year prior.

When I relayed details of the short film, she emanated pride and mailed care packages of candles and clothes to a new apartment in

Brentwood I shared with a roommate. Lori celebrated my wins and believed in me, but shortly after the one-year anniversary of my dad's death, she introduced me to a friend and ex-son-in-law of hers on one of our tri-weekly FaceTime sessions.

"Drew. Drew, come say hi," said Lori, "One sec, he's in the kitchen. He comes from a good family, and oh, here he is..."

Even knowing he was married, Lori nudged me toward dating this East Texas man and urged me to visit over the Fourth of July. In the two months approaching my visit, I locked myself in my room to FaceTime with him every night. My desires faded into the background, falling back into the pattern of making a man the primary focus in my life. Soon, the idea of living near both of them brought immense comfort.

I ignored the inner screams of my intuition and the voiced concerns of Chris, who warned against dating Drew. When Tahmina questioned my reason for moving back to Tyler—*are you sure you want to move, what about your dream?*—I ignored her concern and chased the story-book life, willing myself to believe every word Drew spoke as truth. I changed my number and vowed to not contact Bradley, wanting to give Drew an earnest shot at my fidelity.

During our evening FaceTime calls, I savored every single word this man uttered, even though deep down, a part of me knew they were reverberated lies. He shared promises to marry me while he was married to another woman, to adventure together, to live wild and free. He conveyed how amazing and beautiful I was, how in love he was, and how he would support my writing ambitions. He appealed to my ego, my vanity, and my wounded inner child. He told me everything I'd always wanted to hear from Bradley or any other man. I willed myself to believe him, negating my intuition and inner screams.

I doodled "Kristin loves Drew" in journals, wanting so much to believe that someone's love consumed them like love did me, that I was worthy of the love and the devotion. I had started down the path of valuing myself but abandoned it with the promise of all-consuming love. With my attention placed on Drew, I diverted every ounce of energy away from me and to him. My journal entries from the time are a clear indicator of how we believe the stories we tell ourselves, and how sometimes, life drives you off the bridge to teach you a swimming lesson.

Journal Entry: Tuesday, July 22, 2014.

> So ready to be reunited with Drew. I'm so in love with him, quirks and all. A deep appreciation of him because of past relationships. I promise to be honest and faithful. Free of Bradley's puppet strings. Trying to release the fear of finances. I value myself to not allow or tolerate disrespectful behavior. Appreciate being treated right.

Journal Entry: Friday, August 1, 2014.

> Now that I've met Drew—the ending seems so clear. We experience things and circumstances, however difficult, for a reason. To get to where we are today, we had to go through it first. Also brings a deeper level of appreciation for one another. We value the great more having experienced the bad. He has my heart and while our current situation isn't the most ideal, it will make us stronger. I wish my dad could've met him.

Lust and love pacified and rocked me into a bit of a slumber where I once again doubted my own ability and thwarted my ambitions. The short film proved that I could accomplish what I set out to, but that scared me as well. In a sense, I feared magnificence. The stealth part of my ego craved familiarity and wove it into this tale, a predictable life nestled in the safety and security of Drew and Lori.

> *"All great changes are preceded by chaos."*
>
> —Deepak Chopra

15

DECEMBER 2014

Four months after moving home to Texas, the brilliant Australian sun warmed my shoulders. I jogged down the sandy shore of City Beach in Perth before running straight into the turquoise blue water. A wave crashed into my legs and pulled me under. I surfaced for air and swam past the point of being able to touch. I hopped on my tippy toes and barely bobbed above the water, which felt exactly like my life. I closed my eyes and begged the saltwater to cleanse me, to allow me to stop struggling and float. I wanted to revive myself and release the toxic attachment I held to every man in my life, to mend my broken heart, but I was also afraid of the intensity or pain that may be hidden underneath the dark surface of the water.

I adjusted the bottoms of my black swimsuit as I exited the water. With each step, my toes sunk into the sand, and I thought of the loss prevailing in my life. I missed Lori, who'd succumbed to an addiction to pain pills less than a month after I returned to Tyler. I'd given Drew an ultimatum, and with his divorce unofficial, I'd broken things off with him after three months, which was almost as long as the span of the entire relationship. I mulled over how he'd never believed I'd actually move for him. How the affair was more enthralling and fun with me in California, safely distanced from his life and his wife. I'd once again thwarted myself by heeding the pull of a man. I missed my dad. I missed myself.

I sat down on a green and white striped towel next to Ara, a friend from Perth whom I'd met in an airport a couple years prior. He'd become like a brother to me after he crashed on my couch for weeks at a time when I lived in Dallas. Using money saved from Bradley's continued sporadic wire transfers, I vacationed to visit Ara in an attempt to get over Drew.

Two muscled lifeguards walked past us on the sand with their red trunks, whistles, and buoys.

"Ay, mates, you take a pic with my sis, Kris?" Ara asked.

The two men grabbed my limbs and hoisted me in the air for a photo. The lifeguards didn't give me CPR, but they resuscitated a spark inside me, a remembrance that playful moments can coexist inside all of the pain, if I was open to them.

Stretching across the towel, I dried my hands off before checking a couple emails on my phone, and as much as I dislike admitting, to see if Drew had emailed. I clicked on a message from Colin. I expected to read of his upcoming Christmas plans, or some witty remark about me escaping Texas in December, but the email only included a link to an East Texas news website.

"East Texas Man Arrested For Criminal Solicitation"

I read the name of the man. The same man I'd relocated to East Texas for. The same man who'd shattered my heart with lies. The man I took a damn trip to Australia to get over. The article noted extramarital affairs and mentioned me—not by name, but by a nickname we'd used playfully. Waves of nausea radiated throughout my body. I lowered my head and placed my hands on the ground to brace myself, grounded by the Earth's rotation and simultaneously shot out of orbit.

"Kris, Kris...are you okay?" Ara said.

When I couldn't find the words, I handed him the phone. I laid there with tears streaming down my face and watched him read how Drew had attempted to hire a hitman to kill his wife.

"Fuck. Wow, Kris, you really know how to pick 'em," he said.

"Ara, please."

I rolled over on my back and placed my hands on my head as if to lasso my thoughts into something cohesive. "Fuuuuuuck. I'll just deal with this when I get home," I said.

"If they don't apprehend you at the airport," he said.

I wanted him to stop talking. Everything needed to stop. I needed to breathe. But Ara was a true friend and a teller of the hard truths.

"The article doesn't mention my name," I said.

"Listen, doll. You're out of the country when an ex-lover of yours attempts to hire someone to kill his wife? You need to act on this. This is serious."

I sank into the sand with the realization of a possible implication in the crime and listened to Ara. My hands trembled as I dialed the number from memory, the number of the only person who had ingrained into me that he would be there no matter the circumstance, Bradley. I recounted the details of my location and the situation and forwarded him the news article.

"And this is the type of person you chose to date over me?" he asked.

"You were engaged at the time. *Again*," I said. "I think I might need a lawyer."

"If you think you might need one, then you probably do. I'll make a phone call."

Relief spurted out in an outpouring of cries and tears.

"It's gonna be okay, baby," said Bradley.

"Okay," I said. "Okay."

When I arrived home from Australia, a detective's card was taped to my front door, and within a week or two, my car bobbed up and down over the red brick streets of downtown Tyler on the way to the police department. After parking in the bare lot, I sat in my car for a few deep breaths. My lawyer pulled into the space next to me. The lawyer whom Bradley had retained—whose father had represented and exonerated a prominent Manziel murder case in Tyler—ironically had been contacted by Drew's family for representation. Had I not moved upon Ara's urging, they'd have secured him first.

I stepped out, greeted my attorney, and walked into the light brown police building. We followed the detective through a metal detector into a small room and sat across from him. The detective pressed a button on a handheld recording device between us. "This is Detective Nathan Elliott interviewing in reference to the investigation of Andrew Patrick Olson. Can you please state for the record your full name?"

I felt as if I peered at my life from a bird's eye view. Only this scene didn't feel like my life. As I sat in the fluorescent-lit interview room, my life felt more like an episode on the Investigation Discovery Channel.

"Kristin Nell Birdwell."

"You understand you're willingly cooperating. You're not legally obli-gated to talk."

Except you told me last week after visiting my employer and my apart-ment that if I didn't cooperate, you'd subpoena me to testify in front of a grand jury.

"Yes," I said.

Sweat formed a layer of dew on my palms, the lawyer who sat to my right being the only calming presence. Was I responsible in some way? I'd pressured him to leave his wife. And how was I capable of still hav-ing feelings for a man capable of devising such a sinister plan? Did my attraction to him in turn make me evil?

The detective slid an enlarged photograph across the tiny table. I glanced down and a jolt spiraled my spine. The photo showed my apart-ment complex, or how it would appear if taken through a gun scope. My body relaxed when I noticed the photograph was of my two noisy, upstairs neighbors. I remembered the night.

"What in the world are they doing up there?" I had asked Drew as I glared at my ceiling.

"Only one way to find out," he said.

He grabbed his binoculars and walked to his truck. When he returned, he told me how two men were arguing. He described how one man ate spaghetti on the toilet with the door open while talking to the other shirtless man. After a few more loud stomps above, we threw blow darts at the ceiling in an effort to quiet them down. The detective's voice brought my awareness back to the present moment.

"We found this photo in Andrew's cell phone. Is this your apartment complex?" he asked.

A smidgen of relief rose through me, but I suppressed a smile because of the situation's severity.

"That's my complex, but not my apartment. I live on the bottom floor."

See, Drew isn't that crazy. He wasn't spying on me in the parking lot. The man I'd loved wasn't capable of the accused crime. This couldn't be true.

Detective Elliott looked as if I had kicked him. My lawyer leaned in. "Try to answer with just a yes or no."

"Do you know of any drug use?" the detective continued.

"A prescription for Adderall, Klonopin, ibuprofen," I said.

"Anything else?" he asked, eyebrows lifted in question, as if he knew the answer.

"Methamphetamine."

"Did you see him personally use this drug?"

"Yes," I said, leaving out how I'd smoked the rocky substance with him a couple times. I'd held a glass pipe, watched the white smoke swirl around the bubble as Drew held the lighter underneath. As the drug entered my system, the adrenaline rush matched the energy and the sex-crazed fuel of our relationship. He'd become every bit of a drug. From the look on the detective's face, he assumed I had done the drug anyway.

"Did you know Andrew was married?" Detective Elliott asked.

Shame rose to my cheeks, but truth was my ally. I peeled the words out of my heart and out of the disgust I held for myself. "He'd said a divorce was in the works."

"Do you know that Andrew has another child with someone who isn't his wife?"

"Yes," I said.

"Huh. His wife didn't know about that till I told her. Do you know his wife's name?"

"Yes, Ashley."

"She's scared of you," he said.

"What? You're kidding. I told her who I was after I found out he was lying to both of us. I wrote her a letter that included texts from him and photos of us."

I had wanted to rid myself of him when I sent her the letter, expressing how I wanted to put the "nail in the coffin" of our relationship. Bad word choice given the eventual circumstances, but I didn't know the severity of Drew's intention when he'd wished his wife would just go away. I'd heard jokes and believed a married man might think of his wife as a pain. And vice versa. Drew wouldn't be able to forgive me for outing us to his wife. The reveal severed all ties. I didn't think I'd be able kick my habit of him any other way.

"Did she tell you she apologized for him dragging me into their marriage, that she had been in my position before, and that she 'wasn't the wife she should've been to him?'" I said.

There went the yes or no answers as I justified my actions to the detective and myself. But really, why would I identify myself if I had planned on harming her?

"Do you have a copy of the letter? Ashley mentioned she might still have it."

If she mentioned the letter, why the hell was he asking me all these damn questions that he already knew the answer to?

"Yes," I said as my lawyer opened up a manilla folder and slid him the ten-page letter, a summary printout of my bad relationship decision.

Detective Elliott pressed a button to stop the recording. "That's all I've got for now. I'll be in touch if anything arises."

Moving to escort us outside of the interview room, he said, "Now, if you're contacted by the media..."

"*Woah*, wait a second. *Media?* If I'm contacted by the media, that means someone up here has some loose lips," I said, knowing my name had never been specifically mentioned in all of the articles I'd scoured.

Detective Elliott took a surprised step back as I turned to leave the station. The cold air felt fresh on my skin on the walk to my car. The leaves on the ground rustled in the wind. It'd been two years since the breakdown in my closet, and I'd felt I regressed. *How could I bring the peaceful breeze inside?* As I backed out of the parking space, for a brief moment, the sun peeked between the dreary clouds and danced across the surrendered red, orange, and brown leaves.

I never spoke to the police after that winter day, but Drew would take a plea deal for twenty-five years later that year. The stakes were heightened with this experience—innocent people could have been harmed. With a light shining on how my actions could affect others, I decided to change. I asked myself what type of role I wanted to stand in, what type of impact I wanted to have. The contrast highlighted the areas to change, particularly in relationships, and I figured I needed to start with the one I had with myself.

> *"When you change the way you look at things, the things you look at change."*
>
> —Wayne Dyer

16

True to pattern, within months, I turned outside of myself. This time, to shamans, mediums, and quests to fix what I believed to be the broken parts of my life and to provide guidance for a spiritual awakening. I aligned my chakras with crystal pendulums and scouted solutions from books, Google searches, and personal stories. Per Colin's recommendation, I found myself sitting in a dilapidated shopping center in Garland, Texas, outside of a tiny massage parlor. The bars on the windows didn't point to peace or enlightenment but were an accurate physical representation of my inner life.

I stumbled into the office and sat in a chair across from Anna, a blonde, heavy-set medium. As she closed the flimsy mini blinds in her office window, I pondered how she managed to get a brush through the mountain of frizz sitting on top of her head. I quickly tried to change my thoughts in case she happened to be clairvoyant too. She pushed her glasses up to the top of her short nose.

"I'm sensing a male figure. Yes. A man named Tom," she said.

My eyes darted from the ashes falling beneath an incense stick on a corner table to the inspirational quotes and reiki certificates on the wall before making eye contact with her blue eyes again. Hearing "Tom" straightened my spine. I'd booked the session through Colin. She knew my dad's name without knowing me or even my last name. My inner child rose to the surface, pleading to be seen, seeking comfort and acknowledgment. *Is he really here? Does he still love me? Why did he leave me so soon? Tell me he's proud of me.*

"You ever date someone and then they just stop contacting you out of the blue?"

"Yes," I said.

"He's guiding them out of your life when he doesn't think they're good enough for you."

She looked at the massage table. My eyes followed, squinting to see if I sensed his spirit sitting on the maroon cushion.

"A woman is here too, all done up. Brunette. Dressed to the nines," said Anna.

"Lori," I said, nodding my head in recognition, loving the image of her and my dad wandering the spirit realm together.

"Do you cry alone in bed at night?" she asked.

How did she know these details? I didn't want to claim my sadness.

"It's where I feel the safest to do that, yeah," I said.

"She visits you while you're sleeping. She wants you to keep going. Keep writing, taking classes. Don't put your life on hold for her or for anyone else. Find the inner love and acceptance for yourself that she never found."

The words resonated. I saw myself continuing on a path similar to Lori's, seeking and filling voids with men, drugs, and booze. I didn't want that life.

"Let me see your hand," said Anna.

My fingers trembled as I offered my hand for her to examine. She flipped my hand face up and cupped it in her small, smooth hands. I hoped to hear her spout tales of future financial success and healthy relationships. Anything she uttered would be a delight in comparison to the recent deaths of my dad and Lori. How did one lift the cloud of grief?

A curious line creased her forehead. Her eyes widened with surprise before nodding her head in confirmation, a sly sparkle in her eyes.

"You have what I call alien hands, more lines than me," she said as she peered into the lines of my palm. "You signed up to learn a lot of lessons this lifetime."

I leaned in to stare at the crazy crossings across my left palm and her words resonated as truth. I yearned to know if my lessons were all behind me or exactly how many were still ahead. Were inner peace and happiness destinations I'd finally arrive at? How did I get there? Where was the Waze-like GPS voice of my life, signaling for objects in the road, notifying me when to turn, and alerting me of my arrival? I mean, shit, how many humps were left? At twenty-six, I'd lost my dad to cancer, lost my stepdad to his behavior, lost Lori to an opioid overdose, lost friends, seen two lovers jailed, and lost touch with myself. Why was loss so prevalent in my life? Surely the trajectory was bound to take an upward swing. Where was the flow to this life of ebbs?

I'd come to realize that the voice of guidance resided inside me, that meditation helped me detach from identifying with my fleeting thoughts or situations and instead come to know the deep-seated peace within. I'd learn how my soul communicates through my body. But at this point, I resisted sitting with myself in silence.

I leaned in closer to Anna and cocked my head. She seemed to understand a greater meaning of life. Maybe by being closer to her truth, some of her wisdom would rub off on me. *More, tell me more.* She placed my hand on the table and tapped the backside as if to say, *that's enough for one day.* Her lips formed a gentle smile and glanced at the clock. Our hour-long session was over.

"You're meant to be a healer," she said.

A healer?

For a moment, the concept landed foreign in a pit of resistance. But a vibration rang from deep within, an acknowledgment that her words were true. Was being a healer a part of my path to bridge where I was to where I wanted to be? At the time, I didn't think anyone could be more fucked up than me. I just pretended better. Pretended to be strong and okay, pretended to be happy, ever optimistic, and have my life together, pretended to live a glamorous life not filled with pain and depression. How was I supposed to help others when I couldn't even be honest with myself?

When I left her office, restlessness mounted with the stirring of a possible bigger life purpose to help heal others. Anna had planted a seed. The visit with her activated a longing that'd later evolve into an offering to share my learnings in hopes of helping others heal, helping them learn to love all parts of themselves, helping them find love and liberation in the nest of themselves.

But I'd have to get there first.

So, I asked myself, what had I learned thus far? True happiness didn't reside in anything materialistic. Depression lingered in the richest man

I'd known, so happiness didn't live in the dollar. And I certainly hadn't found the missing puzzle piece of me in another person. Being healed must be more like life itself, more of an unfolding journey than an end-point. The final destination of healing seemed to be a mirage.

Might happiness, or worthiness, not live outside of us, but start *within*? And if joy began within, what else sprung from our inner life? How might I harness the power of my inner life and mind to work for me?

I know now that to change our trajectory and our outcome, we start by focusing on and accepting ourselves. Asking ourselves those brave questions and standing in our truthful answer. Our self-relationship is the most important one, as every other relationship is experienced through the lens of us. When we work our way from the inside out, we have the ability to adjust our emotions and thoughts by selecting ones better suited for our well-being and desires.

After the session with Anna, I sprinkled a bit of compassion into my life with the fresh perspective of viewing my mishaps as learning lessons.

If I approached my experiences, even the most difficult ones, with a curious and grateful heart, the lessons were gifts of redirection or insight. If the lesson from a painful experience was a gift, then the experience itself was a gift—making all of life a gift.

"We're all just walking each other home."

—Ram Dass

17

My focus shifted to personal development, to progressing with living a new life imbedded with awareness and curiosity, and to strengthening my relationship with myself. To do that, I needed to surrender the stories of my past where so much of my identity centered on being a victim, fixated upon what others had done to me. How would I thrive if cinderblocks of shame and blame were cemented to my essence? Was forgiveness a lesson I'd signed up to learn?

Some months after the night in Oklahoma, Lonnie had started drinking again. My instant reaction to the news was guilt. I intellectually knew his decision to drink wasn't my fault, but did him molesting me play a factor in his choice to break a twenty-plus year sobriety streak? Would my forgiveness release him from any pain or guilt? Would that forgiveness free me?

While forgiveness would take time, I focused first on my own honesty. A month or two following the session with Anna, I completed a handwritten book for my mom, detailing the ways in which I was grateful for her, thanking her for the endless support and encouragement over the years, for loving my free spirit, and for never trying to cage me. I wrote how she knew everything about my life except for one situation that I wanted to talk about with her in person—the night at the cabin with Lonnie. I considered ripping the page from the book. But without that heartbreaking page, the book wouldn't be whole.

Would the revelation of Lonnie's actions transfer my pain to my mom and ruin her, anchor her down with scrambled thoughts of what she could've done to protect her daughter? Something inside of me spoke and urged me to press on. I wasn't meant to carry everyone's load. I simply had to get a grip on mine.

Before losing the courage to share my secret, I stuffed the book, its words hinting at a life-changing revelation—one that would liberate me—into her Christmas stocking. I'd wait for an opening to continue the conversation the book started.

Remnants of red, white, and green wrapping paper scraps littered every inch of the tile floor between the tree and the couch where my mom, her boyfriend, Christopher, and I sat in our pajamas on Christmas morning.

"Don't forget to save the bows," Mom said.

After she distributed our stockings, she sat beaming on the cushions and emptied the contents of her stocking onto her lap, the tiny pink book of my scribbles falling onto her thighs. With a jolly, open-mouthed smile, she flipped through the pages. She paused on a page, nodded to herself, and flipped to another one.

"Woo, a tearjerker, Kristin," she said, dabbing her eyes with her long sleeve.

Her boyfriend leaned over to sneak a peek at my words over her shoulder. She shooed him back. My brother examined instructions for a camping device. Mom and I locked eyes and walked outside.

Our feet crunched into the gravel road outside her boyfriend's square, metal home. The trees stood tall and firm in the earth around us. I felt as if they may close in on us at any moment, as if the trees were the ones holding crisp anticipation and secrets in their pine-cones. My emotions whipped back and forth as if they were clothes hanging out on a line to dry, wondering what my mom would do with my dirty laundry.

"Slithered up right there," she said, pointing to a spot in the grass next to the driveway.

"Alright, Annie Oakley. Was it poisonous?" I asked.

Her chin quivered. I understood she wanted to stall my revelation with her story of shooting a snake in the yard with her pink pistol. She faced me with tears lining the rimmed edge of her hazel eyes. My shoulders tensed, bracing for the emotional exposure.

"Please tell me it wasn't your brother," she said.

"Lonnie," I said.

I hugged her, filled in the pieces of the story...shedding my own snakeskin.

"He always tried to protect you. Told me not to leave you alone with certain people. Was so strict with you. And then he goes and does something like this? I'm so sorry."

"It's not your fault," I said.

"I'm so sorry," she said.

Even though I requested her not to, a part of me hoped and knew she'd contact Lonnie. He followed up and apologized for his behavior in a text, said in some way he'd used me to get back at my mom for leaving, but admitted his behavior was unacceptable. I told him I wouldn't have told my mom if I hadn't worked on forgiveness for him.

I let go of the anger and the bitterness and found a thread of acceptance. I released the stories of how he should have acted and squirmed away from my attachment to the story of being victimized. His actions traumatized me once, but I traumatized myself continuously with the relentless repetition of victimization.

With this surrender, I formed a different story, one where I hold immense gratitude and love for Lonnie. And I'd rather hold those emotions than hate. I'd rather use love to fuel my journey than allow resentment to suffocate me. The part of me that wondered how he was could peacefully and simultaneously exist with me never wanting to see him again. Love existed in spaces, not just proximity, and the love for Lonnie lived in the space between nonjudgment and detachment. I didn't have to determine if the experience was bad or good—it could contain neutrality and just be. I could learn and heal. I could move on.

His life philosophy formed much of my foundation. I choose to value the lessons instilled in me growing up that opened a world of possibility in me. I do honor the frightened little girl inside, but finding meaning in the pain helped me grow beyond victimization. He was the first person I decided to love from afar, but not the last.

Forgiveness released the tension held in my jaw and back, cleared weight in my heart, and created space for clarity in my mind. Forgiveness helped me make decisions that supported and delivered me on a path to freedom. I recognized I'd be able to relate to, hold space for, and help others with similar traumatic experiences.

I do believe I signed up to learn a lot of lessons in this lifetime. Because the more lessons I learn, the more I'm able to help and guide others. I walked the path to be a healer by walking the path of healing myself. Forgiveness helped pave the way.

A few months after finding forgiveness for Lonnie, I read about empaths. Author Andre Sólo said, "Empaths see the world differently than other people; they're keenly aware of others, their pain points, and what they need emotionally."

Yes, definitely an empath—which meant I was a people pleaser who could sense the needs of others. Great. People in my life rarely expressed their needs verbally. I felt them through an emotional, clairsentient spidey sense. And with a sense of loved ones' needs and desires, I acted in accordance with my own longing for acceptance and love, not granting them the same sovereignty I desired. I manipulated people in an effort to sway their emotions in favor of loving or accepting me. This insight helped me realize that when neglecting my own emotions, I often sought to nurture the emotions of those around me—which I feel intensely. If my attention was placed on others, guess where it wasn't directed? On me—or on my own wants and needs.

To shake the people-pleasing tendency, I initially attempted to analyze my way out of the behavior. Did a desperate drive to be needed or loved hold me in a pleasing, feigning, leaving cycle? Did keeping Bradley on the back burner align with my conscious pull toward independence or sovereignty? The answer seemed muddled. While the money offered freedom of time, the strings seemed to tether me to an acceptance of lower treatment, ashamed by the lack of belief in myself. Was I ready to surrender our relationship? And were the strings his...or mine?

Bradley owned a sprawling ten-acre estate on Lake Austin, but he split his time between Los Angeles, Dallas, and Austin—migrating to California as the Texas heat and humidity rose and the mosquitoes donned their yearly muscle shirts.

In the year or more since seeing him, I'd focused on my needs and wants. Outside of an occasional dinner date here or there, I dated myself and rather enjoyed the soul-seeking time alone. But a part of me struggled with not feeling desired and my ego rationalized Bradley as the best catch I ever landed, spoke to the doubt of being on my own, and fanned a financial fear flame.

On an early fall evening in 2015, I initiated a reunion. Seeing him would be a progress test of sorts. Would this new me, refreshed with her own desires, voice my needs and emotions to Bradley? Maybe he'd changed. And then there was the thrill of not knowing which version of him would greet me and, let's be honest, the soothing, benzo-like effect of wire transfers.

After our reunion, celebrated with a night of drinking, I slipped out of Bradley's purple downstairs master suite, tiptoeing across the plush carpet past one of his prized crystal guitars encased in glass.

The Keurig churned to life and dribbled liquid gold into a coffee cup. I climbed the gold and black winding staircase to one of the upstairs bedrooms. After showering and wrapping myself in a blanket-sized Turkish towel, I stepped onto the balcony and settled into an iron chair overlooking Lake Austin. A ski boat drove in front of his house, pulling a wake surfer. The sun beamed into the trees, illuminating a golden reflection on the lush greenery of the protected hill-country land. I sipped my coffee, mulling over how my actions differed from what I desired.

I wanted to know the woman I'd become without his financial help. To not only survive, but thrive, outside of his nest of security.

I wanted him to see the greatness I saw in him—his intelligence, his humor, his magnificent storytelling—how I loved the wounded boy who drank his feelings of inadequacy or bottled them for a later expulsion. Yet isn't it ironic how I desperately aimed to convince him of his greatness while struggling to see my own?

I packed my things, and at the last second, tossed the plush towel into my overnight bag.

Walking past the grand piano, I thought of how hours earlier I'd laid naked spinning in a circle on it in the middle of the foyer. From the piano, we'd stood under the outdoor shower. Giggling underneath the stream of water, he'd urged me to talk more, but past a certain point of imbibing, the words faltered and fumbled in my mouth. I now see he also wanted more or a different version of me, but neither of us was ready to bare all and we both craved something the other couldn't seem to give.

Sometime after the outdoor shower, my new intentions washed away and I slipped into old patterns, warming myself next to the fireplace after a cocaine feast and Bradley's raised voice. I had started paying attention to my energetic state around people, and if I didn't enjoy the feeling or feedback of my actions, I told myself I didn't have to stay and could choose to stay away. I'd failed a test with Bradley and slipped into old behaviors like a whiskey rock fitting into a glass.

Walking out the door, I paused for a moment when the hinge creaked. A doe raised her head and looked in my direction before scampering across the lawn with her white-speckled fawn trailing behind. Together, they leaped over the property fence into an adjacent pasture, bounding past the grazing longhorns. *Was I willing to protect myself like a mother would?*

I backed my car out of the garage area and paused for a moment to take in the twenty thousand square foot home, the black Lamborghini, and the gold Bentley positioned in my rearview mirror. Beyond those items were the memories and the ideas of how great we could be together, a fantasy ideal I had held on to for seven-plus years.

I shifted the car into drive and steered away. Along with apologetic text messages for an outburst, Bradley wired $5,000 into my bank account.

Shortly after, I started working as a traveling Product Specialist for BMW—the same position I'd wondered about while touring an auto show during my radio internship years prior. The job helped fuel the belief that I could thrive on my own. The travel required for work helped place space between any weak moments of longing. While on the road, I journaled and released resentments toward Bradley. I'd resented him offering parts of himself, but at that time, I only offered parts of myself. I finally understood how what we offered one another seemed to be conditional love, and in a sense, not true love. The world is our mirror.

Although I'd released a part of me attached to the luxuries and stability he provided and had chosen to love him from afar, I visited him one more time after the night in Austin. I'd changed so much over the two or three years since pulling out of his driveway, and my curiosity, once again, wondered if he'd evolved as well. A part of me questioned if he thought I stayed only for the money. If I was successful in my own right and chose him, well then, he'd know my love, although muddled, was true. And part of me wanted to prove to him and myself that I loved him, not his money. I also wanted to show him how well I was doing. And in a crazy sense, for him to be proud of me, almost like a father.

I understand now, after reading *Getting The Love You Want* by Harville Hendrix, how we subconsciously select partners that hold the positive and negative traits of our primary caregivers in an effort to heal our childhood traumas and rewrite our past story. With the emotional unavailability, charm, and idolization, Bradley seemed to be a mix of my dad and Lonnie. After I passed the initial reaction of wanting to vomit by thinking I'd dated my dads, I accepted the knowledge in the book and approached dating with a deeper awareness.

At the time, Bradley had undergone ketamine-assisted therapy and wasn't drinking. Him showing up for himself gave me hope for the us I'd dreamed about, for the him I knew he could be. But the conversations and silences that last evening with him felt forced and awkward. Sober, neither of us knew how to rekindle our sexual relationship or build fresh intimacy, almost as if we didn't quite fit together when we weren't both lost.

I'd grown miles from the home I'd once found nestled into his shoulder. I'd be lying if I said there weren't a few late-night text or email exchanges since that last night, but any time I chastise myself, I remember to love myself like a mother nurtures, to love me even if visiting or texting seemed like a step backward. I have a deep respect, love, and appreciation for him, and honestly, I like knowing that he's okay. I don't know if I'll ever see him again, but it seems best in this moment to continue loving him from afar.

Ram Dass said we are all just walking each other home. I've struggled to find the words to express the depth of my love and gratitude for him, to honor the time we spent walking one another home. For every time he showed up for me, for the journey in this life together, for how our time shaped who I am today. Despite all the pain we inflicted on one another, I recognize the privilege in the life he provided. I see the opportunities, the ability to say goodbye to my dad, the time, and the healing space. I hope I helped him on his journey too. I allowed him to rescue me so many times, but during our time apart, I learned I could rescue myself. I am happy our paths forked because our separation led me to me.

I began to lean into my own warmth, my own worth. For me to love myself, wounds and all, I'd have to honor my creative longings. Flittering from his nest, the little girl and sacred woman inside would show how wounded wings fly. With presence, and a little play, she could even be the dragon she'd always wanted to be.

"Who looks outside, dreams;
who looks inside, awakes."

—Carl Jung

18

FALL 2017

With each conscious act of forgiveness, I reclaimed a piece of personal power and freedom, exonerating my present moment and future from being repetitiously shaped by my past choices. On this healing quest forward, my journeys inward and outward continued through international travels and electing to take heart-expanding psychedelics.

While living in Dallas, I'd experienced the token bad mushroom trip and had since steered away from hallucinogens. Not surprising, since I'd held a life pattern of avoiding experiences that seemed out of my control. But after reading into research on the use of psychedelics to heal traumas and how mushrooms could be used as an avenue to evolve consciousness, the notion of transforming my mind inspired me to have another psilocybin mushroom experience.

About a year into a new relationship, on a crisp Saturday evening, a group of friends and I huddled around the country kitchen at Javier's eight-acre ranchette sipping cups of mushroom tea from small, colorful cups. I'd familiarized myself with the selective setting recommendation for mushrooms and chose to have the experience in an open home with ample access to nature. Although it was highly recommended to have a guide for the journey, I felt safe within the small circle of friends. The evening started as something of a psilocybin group therapy dance session before unintentionally transforming into a solo transcendent experience.

While waiting for the effects, we pushed the mustard chaise lounge couches to the wall, widening the living room space for a makeshift dance floor. The rules of our game were simple: select an upbeat song and tell the story associated with the choice. After pressing play for the song, no matter what, the six of us were to dance erratically around the hardwood floor. The game offered a chance to get to know one another, to learn a piece of a friend's story, and to feel wildly accepted. The game created a safe space for vulnerability.

Five friends huddled in a semi-circle around me as I contemplated my song selection.

"Okay, got it," I said. "This song will forever remind me of junior high, being dropped off at the movie theater with my best friend, Lyndsay. We'd have one of our dads crank up the volume and play this song as our exit song, envisioning the wind whipping our hair and stepping down from the truck into our glamorous life at Cinema Five in Mt. Pleasant, thinking we were so cool."

As Def Leppard's "Pour Some Sugar on Me" played, surprise danced over their faces, like a body wave at a sports arena, before we all shook our limbs ecstatically, singing the song together with our arms around one another's shoulders.

A friend whose childhood had been marked with violence reminded himself every day of his journey to success while listening to The Notorious B.I.G. in the shower. A Spanish song reminded another of sneaking out to meet her then-boyfriend, her now-husband. We didn't have to know the words to feel the language and emotion on offer.

The laughter faded with the end of the last song, and we traipsed across the sloped yard. My partner held my hand, adding strength to my balance, as we fought gravity on our downhill walk past the pool.

Nestled amongst oak and cedar trees around the fire pit in the hill country outside of Austin, we traded off magic minutes of silence with outbursts of laughter. After listening to the crackling pops of the fire and a distant singing whippoorwill, I followed the hanging tree lights and walked up the hill to the main house to use the restroom. On my way to rejoin them, the fleeting idea to eat more mushrooms passed through my mind. *Might as well maximize the trip inside in every sense.* Unzipping the plastic baggie, I tossed several additional pieces of the dried fungus into my mouth.

I stepped back outside and wrapped a beige and pink cashmere shawl around my shoulders as I leaned my neck to stare at the expansive night sky, feeling as if I were looking into a reflection. As vast as the sky projected into the distance, the same limitless opportunity for expansiveness lay within. Shortly after I consumed those additional mushrooms, the crew decided to turn in for the evening.

With the rise and fall of steady snores to my left, I laid on my back in bed and placed my arms at my side with my palms facing upward. After several minutes of breathing in the pitch-black darkness, I touched my outer left eyelid to determine if my eyes were opened or closed. Yes, closed.

My breath tightened, becoming more rapid and shallow. Fear closed in until from somewhere I heard...*surrender*. Relaxing, I tuned into my breath, and soon, my soul felt like she was flying amongst the stars on a weightless journey through the galaxy, severing ties with all egoic thoughts and earthly matters. In this astral realm, my dad's presence joined me.

Silent tears streamed down my face as intuition registered the energy and I experienced an epiphany. *He had never left.* A slight giggle joined the tears. The anguish from having felt so abandoned and separate was now funny. Laughing at the illusion and what suddenly seemed like a silly thought in the first place, my tears transformed into ones of pure joy, relishing in an equal exchange of healing, unconditional love.

It's all love. Life is the ultimate expression of love, the greatest creativity.

Open and receptive, free-flowing love poured in like I'd never known before, like I'd never allowed. I felt as if I were the love, understood we all were, and how we are meant to offer our unique love and gifts to the world in our chosen, divine expression.

The next morning, after Javier placed a coffee on my nightstand, I sat up with a renewed sense of curiosity and clarity about myself and life. Peace, in an almost indescribable knowingness, how life after death exists and in the knowing my dad had never left. *Was this the inner guide Lonnie had once mentioned?*

I wondered, if for every action, there was an equal and opposite reaction, might this be true for energetic feelings? If so, I had a lot of joy to feel and found hope that on the opposite end of the depression spectrum lived utter bliss and joy. The depth of darkness and pain pointed to how much light and joy could be experienced if I braved the journey between.

While part of me wanted to scream my revelations and insights to everyone at once, I went out to the front porch and observed nature's interconnectedness in silence. With every inhale and exhale, the trees seemed synced and spoke through light waves of their vibrant green leaves sashaying in the wind. Two hummingbirds hovered above a shrub before zipping to rest on a tree branch. A gecko skirted across the Saltillo tile, pausing to display a throat bubbled with air—gifting insight as a reflection into my own throat chakra and the words seemingly trapped in my mouth. *What was holding me back?*

Now I know there was an act of forgiveness left to be made. Months after that inner journey, one rose to the surface while I walked the loop around the neighborhood and listened to a podcast episode with survivors of sexual abuse. A chill of recognition shot up my spine and through the crown of my head when the host asked the guests, "Have you forgiven yourself?"

Tears awaited release from a crime they hadn't committed. Yet they needed recognition and honoring. While I had forgiven Lonnie and Bradley, I'd never explicitly forgiven myself. For feeling naïve. For ignoring my intuition. For manipulating myself and others. For years, I'd spun myself in a web of shame and an internalized notion that I was less than.

Self-forgiveness freed my self-imposed prison and called for me to continue healing and growing. The questions I asked myself began to evolve. Instead of thinking what could be gained out of a situation or how a situation best benefitted me, I asked how I could help others. *How could I serve? How could I give?*

Offering myself forgiveness helped shake victimization and further loosened the pieces of my identity attached to past choices. Claiming responsibility for my actions led me away from believing that one lived solely from life's affects. Awareness began to grow: if I chose, I could affect life...I could co-create with it. If I wanted daisies to bloom, I had to plant daisies within me and my actions. I couldn't just cuss out the roses and kick the weeds, I had to change the seed of me. *What flowers did I want to bloom?*

> *"There is no light without shadow, and no psychic wholeness without imperfection."*
>
> —Carl Jung

19

MAY 2018

My thirtieth birthday began scaring the hell out of me the moment after celebrating my twenty-ninth. I tried to not raise my eyebrows when talking, fearing lines would wrinkle my forehead. I'd stare at my reflection in the bathroom, leaning in so close that the glass often fogged. I pressed down into the natural part of my hair while my eyes bulged at new sprouts of gray. Thirty wasn't *really* old, but I feared aging and losing the appeal of being a twenty-something-year-old, a part of me that I'd worked, objectified, and used for so many years. My ego wanted to keep me safe in old habits or beliefs that assigned currency to beauty.

Despite longing to be loved for who I was on the inside, my authentic self, I'd placed my value and worth in my external appearance. Each passing day brought me closer to what I believed then to be my expiration date. Bradley's former comments or jokes about trading me in for a younger model influenced this belief, as did the societal pressures placed on women through the media.

I'd adopted some of the fear from my mom as well. Growing up, I'd witnessed her use every skin care product under the sun to minimize wrinkles and vocalize how she despised getting older. Growing up, her father, who'd always dated younger women, made comments like, "What would I do with an old woman?" or how women aged like milk and men like fine wine. The shit was in my lineage, and I had doubts about being lovable without the grace of youth on my side.

As the new decade loomed closer, I delved deeper into my fear instead of simply letting a needle dive into my forehead. I shined a light on the shadow parts of me—the areas I denied, hid, or didn't like admitting. While I'm not against a poke here and a prod there, I'd placed the highest value on my beauty and physical appearance—a fading commodity. So much of my identity and worth were wrapped in physicality, but deep down, I knew there was a truer essence even as I feared not having the tool of sex appeal anymore. Granted, physicality was only one thing in my tool belt, but it took up the most space. Like a chameleon, I conformed to others' desires across many realms. *Would I still be lovable if I were to be unapologetically myself, internally and externally?*

And the irony...because the one thing I hated being loved for was the one thing I relied upon most. I'd longed to be appreciated beyond the physical, to be appreciated for depth, to be asked questions about my writing, to be seen and loved for who I am, the light and shadow parts.

But if I didn't have the strength to showcase those, how was anyone else supposed to love the real me? My self-worth needed serious attention and work. I didn't know it then, but we alchemize ourselves by acknowledging the shadow parts, in allowing our full selves to be seen, heard, and held. Building awareness and compassion for the areas we hide or shame allows for transformation like a phoenix regenerates from ashes.

Admittedly, I hoped to expedite the knowing of my true essence in a speed dating type of style. Leading up to my birthday, I listened to guided meditations, practiced yoga, and explored spiritual methods like reiki and sound healing. Bali seemed to be the center of Zen-like places, a perfect place to peacefully roll into my thirties and attempt to welcome change gracefully. The week of my thirtieth birthday, I traveled to Bali for ten days with my mom, my soul sister Traci, whom I'd met days after the detective interview, and Traci's mom. I booked a Balinese excursion that promised to "tap into the energy of my soul and give guidance on how to move forward with life."

The day of my birthday, we trekked to an early morning hatha yoga class perched in a glass and wood birdhouse among the jungle at our resort in Ubud. Traci and I giggled at our moms' side comments during their first class as the instructor adjusted our form and instructed us to hold a pose like we'd hold a baby. When passing my mom, he asked her, "Do you want a healthy baby?"

After class at breakfast, I nibbled off a floating breakfast tray while swimming in the pool. Overwhelming gratitude beamed through my body, feeling pride in how far I'd come and loving the evolution of my relationships, relishing the opportunity to share in my mom's first venture outside of the states. My mom treated us to a day at the spa where we soaked in a rose bath together. As I sat across from her in floating red petals, an appreciation of her encompassed me like the warm water of the tub. I felt as if I'd chosen her, seeing and understanding the balance in how we both inspired and encouraged one another's evolution.

The day after my birthday, the four of us piled into a silver Toyota outside of our hotel. Mudi, our driver, carried us to the home of Luh, our guide for the spiritual expedition to Pura Mengening, a water temple whose name means "stillness." Luh tied a yellow scarf around my midsection, cinching my waist tight, dressing all of us in traditional Balinese sarongs, blouses, and cummerbunds to honor the ritual and cover our shoulders while entering the sacred temple.

Mudi climbed and weaved through the mountains on tight Balinese roads, maneuvering us through ornate rice fields.

"The Americans complain," said Luh, glancing at us from the front seat. "I like to show people the customs and traditions of my people. Show the Bali way. Maybe they'll learn something. In Bali, we always see the lucky side. If my motorbike breaks down today, that's okay, I get to spend more time with my family. Maybe lucky because I'm not able to wreck it. I'm not married. But I'm lucky because I'm able to focus on my business. Maybe my business will bring me a westerner who admires it. We see lucky."

In the midst of mirroring her radiant smile, the comment about Americans resonated and forced a pause. Even while getting ready for the spiritual cleansing, I'd complained about the early wake up time. I decided to change my list of everyday "got to do's" to "get to do's" and to start seeing more of the lucky side of life, like Luh.

Stepping out of the SUV and into a multilevel, lush oasis felt as if I'd stepped into the secret garden—a secret garden where seeds of self-worth and abundance could sprout—a secret garden where one could bloom if they'd trust and allow themselves to surrender, my own type of Eden. I'd expected a touristy crowd, but we were the only people there. I gazed around the temple, enamored by the immaculate greenery and awed by the effort and time dedicated to preparing the offerings for Balinese rituals and customs.

We descended a steep staircase for the water purification ritual. After slipping into a swimsuit and rewrapping the sarong, I dipped my toe into the cool blue water as if to test the water's holiness—could I feel the healing tingle in my toes, was I ready? I knew how cold water transforms and reinvigorates, but did I always want to willingly submit to the uncomfortable? In a word, no, but the weight of inauthenticity finally outweighed the pounds of uncomfortable change.

My mind wandered to breakfast before thinking how Traci had joined the ceremony despite Luh's warning against participating during a woman's moon cycle. My perfectionistic tendency, an overcompensating behavior for believing in my inadequacy, popped into mind. Would the purification still work if Traci bent the rules? Was my intention enough?

A year prior, I'd read *The Untethered Soul* by Michael Singer, one of the most profound and life-changing books I'd ever read. The book taught me that I am not my swirling, anxious thoughts or emotions. I'm the deep-seated awareness observing the two. Since completing the book, I practiced noticing when my thoughts wandered and pivoted back to the present moment. I wanted to be 100 percent present for the purification ceremony.

We formed a semi-circle in front of the water pool designated solely for women. Delicate pink and yellow flowers rested on a small, intricate banana leaf in our hands. We proceeded one by one to lay the offering and an incense stick on the lush, green landing in the center of the four waterspouts.

Standing solemn and silent, Luh's sister sang a delicate song of respect to the Hindu Gods and Goddesses. Traci, her mom, and my mom walked before me, guiding the way through the cleansing ritual, placing their heads under the first spout before moving to the next. Droplets of water splashed onto me as I inched closer. The fabric wrapped around my body felt claustrophobic, the pressure of the water adding extra weight to carry. I lingered in the feeling for a moment, as if to say goodbye to the comfort of the me I'd always known: a big goodbye but also a huge welcome, like I was in the womb, unsure what followed the rush of water.

When I lowered my head under the first waterspout, the sudden gush of water stole the air from my lungs. Persevering under the force, I longed to be fortified for regeneration and to be filled with inner wisdom and power.

"Release what no longer serves you," Luh said.

Luh may need to pick me up tomorrow because I may need to spend the night under this spout.

Moving to the next waterspout, I set the intention to surrender the beliefs and behaviors that no longer served. I visualized the traits floating out of my being, transported by little hot air balloons. The balloon baskets held my people-pleasing tendency, my desire to conform for acceptance, my fears of aging, my doubts of worthiness, my inhibiting perfectionism, my harsh self-judgment, and my inauthenticity—and lifted each trait upward to be transformed for healing.

When surfacing for air after the last spout, I faced my mom, who stood huddled in a three-way embrace with Traci and Kelly.

"I just saw your dad," she said.

Sobbing, I waded through the water to hold her and to be held within our divine sisterhood.

The water cleansed my soul and allowed me to experience the ritualistic harmony that one may experience in a Southern Baptism. So much so that when I woke in the jungle hotel the next morning, I expected the renewed lightness of my spirit that I found the previous day to greet me with the fervor of the cicadas—but I had slipped into a familiar groan. The realization hit that my journey of self-worthiness, love, and acceptance would be a continuous, conscious process. Just because I'd chosen myself one day didn't make the decision true for all the rest of my days. I'd have to choose me every single day. The task loomed, daunting, but I decided I was worth the work.

What I've learned is the spiritual journey isn't a destination I arrive at, but seems to be more of a winding spiral that offers new perspectives at different points along the way. This perspective helps to welcome all the fresh insights and tools on the journey instead of feeling like I am crisscrossing over the same point I thought I'd healed. I don't think I realized exactly how much personal value I'd placed on my appearance or what impossible standards I'd held myself to until examining the beliefs more closely. While I didn't want to admit fears or shadows, simply naming helped dissolve them. Giving a fear or belief power over me was also a choice.

The tool I'd held onto doubled as a defense mechanism against intimacy because allowing people to see the real me required vulnerability. If I was who everyone else wanted me to be, I risked no real rejection. That ego tool of nondisclosure kept the shadow areas "safe."

My decision to not people-please necessitated an embodiment of the most authentic version of myself and a shift deeper toward finding worthiness within. I'd need to check in with myself to see what I wanted, not go with the flow of man or how things had been done before. That river had left me up creek and the paddle had made me think I didn't know how to swim. When sensing another person's emotions, I'd ask myself, "Where is the desire for my actions originating? Does the behavior align with my needs and truth?" I adopted a bit of a policy I'd once heard and admired: "If the response isn't a hell yeah, it's a no."

Vulnerability is beautiful, albeit emotionally "risky." We may feel pushed into unknown territory, but doesn't all beauty arise from what was once unknown? The truth is, we warm ourselves with vulnerability through creating the connection to ourselves and others. Being open helps heal the shame—my own, and what I had taken on as mine from others. I've since witnessed how deeper connections form with the raw exposure of myself and how my sharing liberated others, gifting them the safety and permission to do the same. And while bearing my truest essence still terrifies me at times, I look forward to finding a rhythm and allowing the process to become second nature over time.

What I once resisted revolutionized my growth. We lose or say goodbye to parts of ourselves because it's only when we take a step into the unknown that we're able to welcome a more supportive idea or belief that we may have been incapable of imagining in the former headspace. I lost one belief to gain a new—somewhat foreign and unknown, yet empowering—one. I chose a contrary thought and action to welcome in connection and love with myself and others. Saying goodbye to a part of ourselves, or to an idea we have held, is like a little death. I grieved the old version of me, the one I'd held onto that brought immense comfort and security. I also celebrated the life lived as the former self because all the experiences led to a place to welcome in vigor and purpose. The death of a former self bred space for a new one to grow. In essence, loss welcomed new life, and what I'd come to realize is that I'd awoken the true, sleeping beauty within.

"To thine own self be true."

—William Shakespeare

20

The psychedelic journey helped me release and reroute. The Bali baptism helped me connect to the core of who I am and begin the process of unraveling everything I wasn't. What did I still do only for others? What did I want to do for me?

After returning from Bali, I started working as a field marketing manager for Bacardi. The position didn't require an office and allowed me to mentor others, but the job didn't register as my true north or my soul's sacred expression. The salary and benefits offered another safe, reasonable choice. But I was learning that I didn't come to float on a ball in the middle of a vast Universe for safety or to die a slow death for patriarchal habituation. I came here for expansive evolution in this human experience, for creativity, and for the revival of the divine feminine. Every now and then, I'd pick up my computer to write a blog post or scribble in a spare notebook, but intuition told me my story wasn't quite ready to tell. On an utter leap of faith in the spring of the following year, after realizing I'd never feel 100 percent ready, I quit the draining full-time job.

I booked a reoccurring commercial acting job and followed my interests. I explored sound healing with a crystal bowl workshop and group meditations. I enrolled in Lightworker Academy, an online course guided by spiritual teacher Alyssa Malehorn "specifically designed for healers, soul-based business owners, and anyone feeling the call to expand their consciousness into higher light realms while upgrading their path of service to others." I researched yoga teacher trainings, something I once notated to myself in a morning page session.

And there's truth to the old saying, "When the student is ready, the teacher appears." Patsy, from years prior, walked me through the program details for the yoga teacher training she was leading in Tulum through Black Swan Yoga with a fellow teacher, Christine. Having Patsy as a lead instructor felt like kismet and spoke to the synchronicities in life—how lives intertwine and how she was meant to be in my life in a pivotal way. And for the training to be in Tulum, the same area I'd first traveled to with Bradley, now feeling light-years from the girl who'd ventured there, it seemed as if I would step into a vortex and come out the other side metamorphosized. My intuition knew the training would be transformative.

Patsy's energy had always entranced me. Her words matched the knowing of my inner wisdom that believed the training would be life changing. The training finale would include leading my own yoga class. When I thought of speaking and instructing a group, a lump of discomfort grew in the pit of my stomach while I unconsciously hiked my shoulders, holding the tension up to my ears. But everything I wanted seemed to be on the other side of the rattling fear. *Maybe I need to acknowledge the fear of financial risk and the fear of owning my power by saying goodbye to a version of me.*

A day before my thirty-first birthday and a month before the training was to begin in Tulum, my fingers wobbled when I punched in credit card information to secure my space with a $500 deposit on the $4,500 investment. Later that same afternoon, my partner's trusted friend and business manager left to start a carbon copy of their company—taking another employee and more than half of the business with him. Javier, an immigrant, had poured his life and soul into the company and trusted his partner to run and act in the best interests of the company.

After receiving the news, he kneeled on the brown hardwood floor in front of me. "Postpone your training. I'll pay for it. I need you here. Please. Marry me," he said.

Marry? Was he offering marriage to get me to do what he wanted?

I stood frozen, silently begging him to stand and rewind to the moment before asking me to abandon myself. But had I abandoned myself? I'd joked and pressured about marriage on occasion, but in that moment, I realized I'd wanted primarily to shift his unwillingness. I didn't want to have a traditional marriage with him—rather, I wanted my old pattern of being deemed worthy of marriage, to be deemed worthy of love.

Mind blown and shocked, I saw myself in the desperate plea of his eyes. He tugged at my hand and pulled on my fear of abandonment and lack of security. I'd planned to put the training on a no-interest credit card and pay the balance over the next year. Weighing out the investment, I teetered on staying to help him, to delay the training and allow him to pay...longer than I like to admit.

"Get up, babe," I said. *Please, get up.*

As he stood, every ounce of my being screamed within, begging to not be abandoned again. The divine woman rattled the chains, bellowed who I could be, who I am. Staying for him and delaying my training rang as too deep of a self-betrayal. I knew my actions would likely wound my partner, but I also felt if I stayed, I'd wound myself and grow to resent him. My need to pursue the training, to place priority on a deeper need, finally outweighed the rushed desire to rescue. And even if it meant acquiring debt, I needed to pay for the training. His offering to pay felt like a test of my growth. Had I really evolved if I denied my longing to please and to heed the pull of a man and his money, even if the man was one who treated me with kindness and respect? Had I evolved if I chose his needs above the ones crying from within?

"I need to do this for myself. I hope you understand, I have to go," I said.

I'd come to learn paying for the training was an investment in myself that helped confirm a belief in myself. The choice and money exchange resounded a loud *I believe in you. You are worthy.* Although Javier's and my relationship didn't survive, I learned choosing to prioritize my needs and sovereignty didn't mean I didn't love him. Choosing me meant I loved myself and would increase my capacity to love and show up for others.

———————

The only thing I've never liked about beds was getting out of one. So, a month later in Tulum, when the alarm bell of my phone rang before the rooster cock-a-doodled, I hit snooze twice before rolling out and plopping my feet onto the bare floor. Traci and Phoebe, my roommates for the training, slept, but I needed fuel for the twelve-hour day ahead.

I followed the smell of coffee downstairs to the kitchen of the Airbnb villa where I'd elected to spend the next sixteen days to further learn the ins and outs of vinyasa and myself. I tipped the white Mr. Coffee to pour, but the pot only released a single droplet of dark brown liquid into the beige mug.

I opened and closed drawers of the villa and groaned until I found a filter. I trudged back into bed to journal for a few minutes before heading to the opening yoga flow session with the twelve other women on this intensive journey.

On the way to the rooftop deck, I took the stairs two at a time. A hot humidity caressed the spandex of my lilac leggings further against my body. Leaning over the raised edge of the rooftop, I saw stray dogs digging through trash hoping to find a morsel of food. The air smelled as if the skies were going to pour a thunderstorm at any moment.

After spying an opening in the back row, I rolled out a squishy green yoga mat. When a woman needed to squeeze in the same row, I hurriedly rearranged my yoga mat to allow space. *Would I step up for myself in a way that mimicked the quickness I offered help to others?*

A soft breeze whipped my hair and kissed my skin. The birds sang their sweet morning song, further amping my morning irritability. My soul was ready for transformation, but my body and emotions spoke to the discomfort of impending change.

"Gooooood morning, ladies," said Patsy.

It took everything in me not to roll my eyes.

"You know, sometimes we go through life and the poses with such a poo face," she said. "Check in with yourself. Are you holding yourself in the light of perfection? What standard are you holding yourself up to? And whose?"

My left quadricep burned for relinquishment as I held steady in a low lunge for a warrior II pose. My arms quivered up and down, struggling to hold in a T. As I watched the bobble, I realized I'd held myself to all standards other than my own, including a standard of perfection I'd placed on myself compared to others. The perfectionism, born from a place of not feeling good enough or not believing in my inherent worthiness and pounded into me by our culture, had created a relentless drive to do, attain, accomplish. An infinite amount of "should dos."

The perfectionistic warrior kneeled to battle and surrendered into child's pose on the ground. I wrapped my arms around my upper body and held myself. My own gentle touch landed on my back, new and foreign, but welcome. When my fingertips grazed my shoulder blades, every ounce of my attention landed on myself, guiding my energy home and retrieving the cords attached outside of myself. *When was the last time I'd shown myself kindness? Or been gentle? Touched my skin with a loving caress?* I tapped a pat of appreciation and grazed my fingers along the tender areas of my upper back as if to tell my body, *I'm here, I've got you. I promise not to leave you.*

On the edge of radical self-acceptance, I froze and unconsciously held my breath, until Patsy's warm, loving palm met my lower back and her words gave me permission for a release.

"Let it go," she said. "Let it go."

Strangled sounds of pent-up emotions escaped, surrendering and exhaling the years of self-rejection. Edging to the surface for release, the sobs shed the girl who sought and strived, the one who didn't appreciate the present, the one who lived in an analysis of past choices or anxious thoughts of the future in an effort to control and stifle fear, who acted from her head instead of her heart. Releasing expectations and judgments,

I fell into an inner loving embrace, a deep nurturing of myself that I'd never experienced. I had never thought to gift myself grace.

Not only was my awareness back on myself; I recognized the choice in how to guide the energy with intention. Vowing to practice the art of being, I spread my limbs out wide to shavasana. I'd sought what I hadn't offered myself—love. What I offered the world, I needed to offer to myself first. I rolled onto my left side in a fetal position before sitting up and birthing myself into a new life as a woman with self-compassion and self-love.

"The lotus flower lives in the mud and the muck before blossoming," said Patsy. "Sometimes, we water with the rain, and sometimes, with the salt of our tears."

Her pinkies and thumbs touched to form a lotus mudra before she lowered the mudra to her solar plexus. Our eyes met before she bowed her head and said, "Namaste."

After the flow, I splashed water on my face before joining the group of women to discuss traits of a yogi over a breakfast prepared by a local resident and chef, Manny. I switched back and forth from the plate of food to scribbling notes in the teacher manual. The ladies shouted characteristics until the chatter lulled.

"Any other values?" Patsy asked.

A hummed tightness wrapped a choice around the inside of my neck, offering both the urge to stifle and the need to express. While I held desires in all aspects of my life, I'd rarely voiced them aloud. My voice shook with rawness, as if the words were cracking my truth out of its protective eggshell.

"Authenticity," I said. "Allowing yourself to be seen as who you unapologetically are."

"Honey, that's what you're doing right now," a fellow yogi student said.

I felt a slight tremble in my jaw. Instead of rushing to cover the shake, I greeted the emotions, the tenderness, and the woman whom I'd neglected for decades. Collectively, one could argue, she'd been neglected for centuries.

The next morning, I woke with a lightness in moving forward with more ease and self-support. Manny, the chef, looked at me, handed me a clean plate, and said, "You are happy today."

While I was in my own world the previous day, he'd seen and felt me. This small interaction spoke to an impact my energy has and how it affects the world around me. If someone felt me while I awakened from a world of my own hate, what impact could I have when true and alive?

Sitting on the couch for a lecture, I opened the manual and turned the book back and forth, looking to find the place where I'd left off. I chuckled at how accurate a representation it was: in my frazzled state, I'd written the notes upside down in my teacher's manual. I flipped the manual, righted the world with a little humor and self-compassion, and started a new page.

Father's Day typically signified a bitter, painful reminder of my dad's death, stirring lack, especially if I scanned social media shout outs, and tickling the longing for what I'd wished were different for so many years. Despite progressing into more well-being over the years, I still not only dreaded that Sunday but braced myself for the days leading up to it as well. But on the eve of this Father's Day, my yoga teacher-training graduation day, I found myself so appreciative for my dad, joyful to have had someone so special in my life to miss, a deep gratitude and understanding in the privilege of having a dad I'd known and got to miss. Offering myself compassion and acceptance reciprocally extended to him as I chose to celebrate the time we had together.

The day landed, momentous, aligned with a marker of my own healing. The synchronicity was a sign, like a little wink from the Universe. I interpreted the significance to mean that he was with me and always would be, confirming again what I'd experienced on the psychedelic journey—that our relationship offered growth beyond the death of his physical form.

Sitting for a final gratitude circle with the yogis, the memory from one of my dad's hospital stays came to mind—how he'd nudged me to become a nurse. And instead of perceiving his words as a rejection, I understood my dad had seen me for who I am—a healer. He'd offered suggestions from his wheelhouse, not the holistic, spiritual, written ones of my chosen methods.

A loving warmth radiated from my body as I realized my self-rejection had mirrored back as an unwillingness to embrace acceptance from others. My dad had loved and accepted me for who I was. He'd even seen a truth in me that I hadn't quite discovered. Yet, through my grief and the physical loss of him, I found my healing modalities. He'd helped me become who I was meant to be.

Words I once hated to admit, I now say with a grin: *Daddy was right.* The surest way to get somewhere isn't the quickest. What I'd sought was within. I'd just taken the scenic route to awaken to my true essence. Love had lived in the nest of me all along.

Acknowledgments

Thank you, Mama, for always believing in and supporting my free-spirited ambitions.

Thank you to Mary Nelligan for your honesty and helping me kill the darlings with kindness. This book wouldn't be what it is today without your keen editing, insights, and advice.

Thank you to Sara Connell for helping illuminate and work through writing fears.

Thank you Miguelito and Olinca for providing support and the healing writing space.

Thank you to Ayo Ogunseinde and Daniel Nguyen for author photoshoots that made me feel like a badass.

Thank you to Sophie Kish for guiding me to shatter limiting beliefs.

Thank you to Ruby Fremon for your mentorship while gearing up to publish. Your guidance helped me own who I be.

Thank you to the team at Scribe: Bianca Pahl, Chelsea McGuckin, Skyler Gray, Erin Michelle Sky, Tashan Mehta, Simon Kerr, Caroline Hough, and Marie Kuipers for helping birth my book baby.

Thank you to Mahesh Sriram for brainstorming and drawing the cover vision on a napkin for me.

Thank you Royal, Traci, Kristen, and Tahmina for being such supportive and encouraging early readers.

Thank you Talitha, Don, and Christopher. Thank you for always loving me and giving me shit when I need it.

Thank you, "Bradley." Your kind words of support for the telling of this story blew me away. I'm ever grateful for the journey we shared.

Thank you to all who are woven into these life stories...and those to come.

And last, yet definitely not least, thank you to every reader, for giving my story a chance.

Connect with Kristin

www.kristinbirdwell.com
Instagram: @kristinbirdwell_
Twitter: @kristinbirdwell

Made in the USA
Coppell, TX
04 August 2022